DA 0...  from Stock
                  Libraries

*Leabharlanna Atha Cliath*
BALLYMUN LIBRARY
*Invoice : 05/610  Price EUR12.00*
*Title: Introduction to the a*
*Class:* ~~720.94192~~   720.9472

AN INTRODUCTION
TO THE ARCHITECTURAL
HERITAGE *of*

COUNTY
ROSCOMMON

AN ROINN COMHSHAOIL, OIDHREACHTA AGUS RIALTAIS ÁITIÚIL
DEPARTMENT OF THE ENVIRONMENT, HERITAGE
AND LOCAL GOVERNMENT

# Foreword

The NIAH Interim County Survey of County Roscommon is one of a series to be produced by the National Inventory of Architectural Heritage (NIAH) and broadly follows the format of Counties, Kildare, South Dublin, Meath, Leitrim, Wateford and Wicklow. The NIAH is a state initiative managed by the Department of the Environment Heritage and Local Government. It aims to promote the appreciation of, and contribute to the protection of, the built heritage by systematically recording that built heritage on a nationwide basis.

The purpose of this Introduction to the Architectural Heritage of County Roscommon is to highlight a representative selection of structures in Roscommon, and raise an awareness of the built heritage of the county as a whole. The Introduction is broadly chronological and identifies structures ranging from the medieval abbey at Boyle, to modern day buildings, such as Boyle's St Joseph's Roman Catholic Church.

The fieldwork carried out by the NIAH, in the summer of 2003, covers just over four hundred sites, structures and groups of structures. It must be noted that neither the Survey nor the Introduction is fully comprehensive; they comprise only a sample of the post 1700 structures that can be found in the county.

The NIAH survey of the Architectural Heritage of County Roscommon can be accessed on the web at *www.buildingsofireland.ie*

This allows for the examination of the records in conjunction with the corresponding images. It is intended that this initial survey will encourage an appreciation of the wealth of architectural heritage in the county.

NATIONAL INVENTORY *of* ARCHITECTURAL HERITAGE

Ballymun Branch. Tel. 8421890

# Introduction

The inland county of Roscommon, part of the province of Connacht, is bounded on the west by Sligo, Mayo and Galway and on the east by Leitrim, Longford, Westmeath and Offaly. Much of the county boundary is water: the River Shannon forms the entire eastern boundary, and its tributary, the River Suck, a considerable portion of the western *(fig. 1)*. The name Roscommon (Ros Comáin) is derived from St Comán, marking his foundation of a monastery on a wooded site, c. 540 A.D. The north of the county was included in the traditional lands of the MacDermots, while the south formed part of the territory of Uí Máine, ruled by the O'Kellys. It is one of the few counties where some of the native land-owners remained in possession of their lands after the Cromwellian period of the mid-seventeenth century.

The county is part of the central plain of Ireland and is largely underlain by Lower Carboniferous limestone. However, in the north lies a narrow band of Old Red sandstone as well as a swathe of depleted coal-bearing Upper Carboniferous limestone, which continues northwards into Leitrim and Sligo. The landscape of the county mainly comprises a gently rolling countryside, with sizeable areas of level ground; hill and mountain land is more or less confined to the northern extent, chiefly the Curlew Mountains. There is a distinctive rolling drumlin topography to the north and east of the county, while extensive peat-lands are a feature of the north-west *(fig. 2)*. There is a profusion of lakes along the Shannon north and east of the county, most significantly Lough Allen and Lough Ree.

*(fig. 1)*
MAP OF COUNTY
ROSCOMMON

The mighty River Shannon forms the whole of Roscommon's eastern boundary and the River Suck forms part of the western margin. There are four major lakes: Lough Key, Lough Gara and Lough Allen in the north and wide-spreading Lough Ree in the east.

*Drawn by Matthew Stout.*

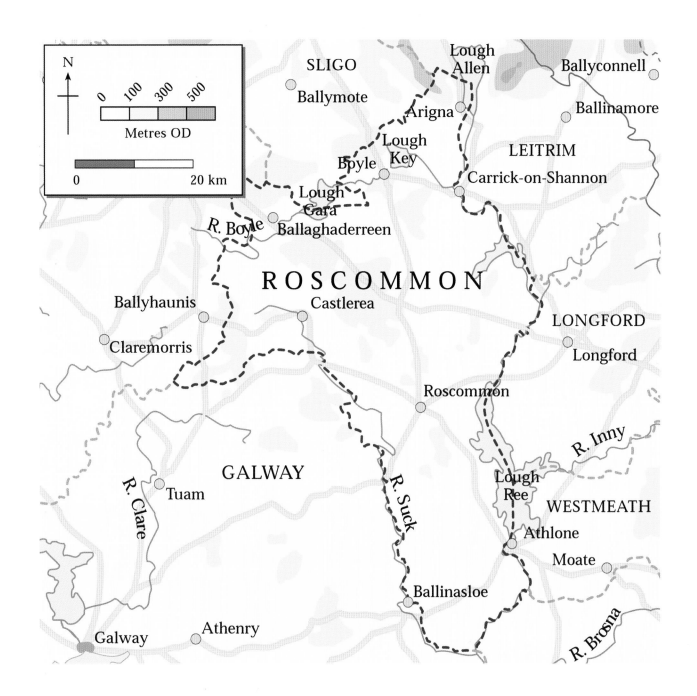

N

0  100  300  500
Metres OD

0                    20 km

SLIGO

Ballymote

Lough
Allen

Ballyconnell

Arigna

Ballinamore

Lough
Key

LEITRIM

Boyle

Carrick-on-Shannon

Lough
Gara

R. Boyle

Ballaghaderreen

ROSCOMMON

Ballyhaunis

Castlerea

LONGFORD

Claremorris

Longford

Roscommon

GALWAY

R. Inny

R. Clare

Tuam

R. Suck

Lough
Ree

WESTMEATH

Athlone

Moate

Ballinasloe

Galway

Athenry

R. Brosna

*(fig. 2)*
This aerial view of
Roscommon just north of
Boyle showing Lough Key.
The county is very low-
lying, the highest land
being less than 600ft
(180m) above sea level.

*Courtesy of the Ordnance
Survey of Ireland.*

Despite the large area of peat and the poor drainage of much of the land, the economy of the county has primarily been agricultural. In the main, the land has been devoted to grazing, with cattle dominating in the north (especially around the fertile plains of Boyle), and sheep in the south. Coal-mining in the mountainous district of Arigna in the north of the county was of major significance for many years. Mining commenced as early as the fifteenth century but the earliest coherent venture seems to have been the establishment of an iron foundry in 1788, where the local coal was used in the smelting process. This particular speculation proved unsuccessful, but coal-mining continued through the nineteenth and twentieth centuries until finally ceasing in 1990.

As is common throughout Ireland, many of the towns and villages originated as fording or bridging-points on rivers, for defensive reasons and as good locations for religious settlements or mills. In Roscommon, the most significant of these are Boyle and Castlerea, which evince different formal characteristics: Boyle is an old settlement with a medieval abbey and bridge, whereas Castlerea is a later, strongly ribbon-type settlement. Strokestown is a very different type of town again. It was laid out in the early nineteenth century by the local landlord, Maurice Mahon, first Baron Hartland (1738-1819), according to a formal plan. Its long, broad main street, terminated by the gates to the demesne, creates a striking and grand vista.

# Pre 1700

Evidence of early settlement can be found at Rathcroghan, near Tulsk, a complex of over fifty archaeological monuments, ranging from the Neolithic to Early Christian periods *(fig. 3)*. The site of Cruachain, the ancient royal capital of the kingdom of Connacht, is reputed to have been the residence of the mythical Queen Maeve. The focus of the site, a flat-topped circular mound, has been suggested as a royal inauguration site. Most famous is the cave known as Oweynagat, 'the cave of the cats', a site steeped in mythology and folklore as an entrance to the 'otherworld'. A man-made stone-lined passage leads to a long cave naturally formed in the limestone bedrock. One of the lintels at the entrance is a re-used fifth-century ogham stone.

At the county town of Roscommon, the monastery founded around the year 720 by St Comán does not survive today, but there are ruins of a Dominican priory founded by Felim O'Connor, Lord of Roscommon, and consecrated in 1257. Only a few years later, in 1269, an extensive castle was commenced just to the north of Roscommon town, by Robert de Ufford, the King's Lord Justice in Ireland *(fig. 4)*. A keepless castle, the quadrangular structure comprised four corner towers linked by an immense curtain wall. The castle passed into Irish hands in 1276 when it was taken over by Hugh O'Connor. For the next three hundred years the castle mostly remained in the possession of the O'Connors. In 1569 the Lord Deputy, Sir Henry Sidney, finally secured the county and nine years later Roscommon Castle was granted to Sir Nicholas Malby, the Queen's Governor of Connacht. Malby carried out extensive alterations, most distinctively the insertion of a number of large mullioned windows.

*(fig. 3)*
**RATHCROGHAN**
**Tulsk**

Long recognised as one of the 'royal sites' of Ireland, comparisons have been made between Cruachain and Tara, and also with Tailteann, Dún Ailinne and Eamhain Mhacha. There are more than twenty ring forts, burial mounds and megalithic tombs in a very extensive archaeological landscape.

*(fig. 4)*
**ROSCOMMON CASTLE**
**(Mid to late-thirteenth century)**

Located on a hillside just outside the town, Roscommon Castle is quadrangular in shape; it has a D-shaped tower at each corner, three storeys high, and a twin-towered entrance gateway. The gatehouse here is amongst the largest in Ireland and the corner towers were able to accommodate a number of spacious chambers. At first floor level they are equipped with fireplaces and latrines. A large house was added by Sir Nicholas Malby about 1580, utilising the north curtain wall.

*(fig. 5)*
**DESERTED VILLAGE**
Rindoon

Rindoon is without doubt one of the finest examples of a deserted medieval town in Ireland. It is situated on a promontory, extending into Lough Ree, midway between Athlone and Roscommon Town. Since the decline of the site after the fourteenth century it has returned to pasture and today the ruins of the castle, harbour, town wall, two ecclesiastical sites and a windmill are visible. The surviving remains constitute one of the most important complexes of medieval monuments in the country.

*(fig. 6)*
**BOYLE ABBEY**

Aerial view showing the quadrangular layout. Boyle is the most attractive of the Irish Cistercian churches and stylistically the most intriguing. The combination of Burgundian and English characteristics is especially interesting. It was built over a long period, which gave rise to several changes of design.

The deserted town of Rindoon is sited on the peninsula of St John's Point, on the west side of Lough Ree *(fig. 5)*. It was occupied by the Anglo-Normans in 1227, at which date the castle was erected. The extensive remains of the town include several houses, the castle and church and the Hospital of St John, as well as the defensive wall, built to protect the settlement from the landward side. It was abandoned in the fourteenth century.

Like Roscommon town, Boyle owes its existence to the foundation of an abbey *(figs. 6-7)*. A daughter house of Mellifont, Boyle Abbey was founded in 1161 and was finally consecrated in 1218. It is one of the finest Cistercian sites in the country. The complex was constructed in several campaigns, resulting in a confusing diversity of styles. Nevertheless, it follows closely the layout of all Cistercian abbeys, with the buildings centred

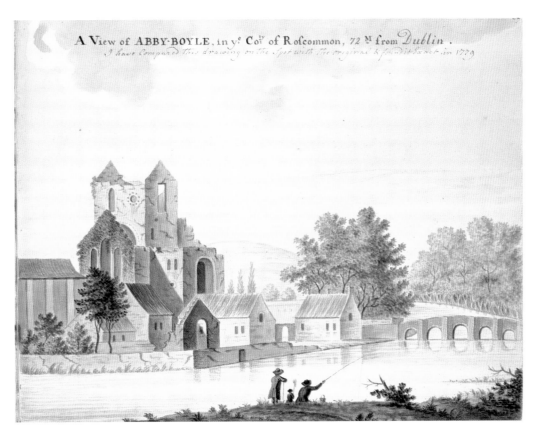

A View of ABBY-BOYLE, in y.e Co.ty of Roscommon, 72 M. from Dublin.
I have compared this drawing on the spot with the original & found it exact in 1779

*(fig. 7)*
**BOYLE ABBEY**

'A View of Abby-Boyle in ye: Co:ty of Roscommon, 72 M: from Dublin'
Watercolour sketch by Gabriel Beranger, c. 1779.

*Courtesy of the National Library of Ireland.*

*(fig. 8)*
This view from the south arcade shows inserted corbels (c. 1215) and the change in the design of the arches. The piers in the south arcade (c. 1180) are cylindrical in plan whereas those in the north (c. 1200) are clustered.

(fig. 9)
'Abbey Boyle Co: of Roscommon'
Looking east down the nave. Drawing by the Reverend Joseph Turner (1772-1835) dated 1794.

*Courtesy of the National Library of Ireland.*

around a rectangular cloister garth. The detail of the church is particularly interesting: the different styles demonstrating the transition between the Romanesque and the Gothic. The rich decorative carving of the capitals, which incorporate a variety of floral motifs as well as animal and human figures, is a significant departure from the traditional austerity of Cistercian architecture *(figs. 8-9)*.

(fig. 9)
'Abbey Boyle Co: of Roscommon'
Looking east down the nave. Drawing by the Reverend Joseph Turner (1772-1835) dated 1794.

*Courtesy of the National Library of Ireland.*

The foundation of the abbey was followed between 1190-1220 by the construction of Abbeytown Bridge over the Boyle Bridge *(fig. 10)*. It is a five-span stone arch bridge, mainly of locally occurring sandstone with some limestone. On the upstream face there are massive triangular cutwaters which extend as high as road level and are capped by flat stone slabs. A substantial and fine bridge, it seems never to have been widened or rebuilt.

Some other pre-1700 structures that survive have been much adapted or incorporated into later buildings. Dunamon Castle was originally built c. 1400; it was then extended in c. 1670 and 1700, and underwent further alterations in 1855. The settlements and subsequent rebel-lions of the sixteenth and seventeenth centuries necessitated the construction of 'strong-houses' to protect land holdings. Part of the fabric of one of these survives in Castle Coote House, an eighteenth-century residence constructed within a seventeenth-century 'star-fort'-type house *(fig. 11)*. Francis Grose in his Antiquities of Ireland (1791) suggests that the original house was built by Sir Charles Coote, who was granted a large possession of land and appointed Provost Marshal of Connacht in 1605, in return for his service to the King in the Nine Years War. His fortified house would have asserted his authority and helped secure his lands.

*(fig. 10)*
**ABBEYTOWN BRIDGE**
Boyle
(c. 1200)

View of the Abbeytown Bridge, with corbelled arches, leading to Boyle Abbey in the background. The piers in the immediate foreground belong to the last campaign of construction (c. 1215-20).

*(fig. 11)*
**CASTLE COOTE HOUSE**
**Castlecoote**
(c. 1770)

Castle Coote House
consists of an eighteenth-
century house incorporat-
ing parts of a seven-
teenth-century artillery
fort. Two of the original
flanking towers are
incorporated into the
main house.

# The Eighteenth Century

Following the long years of rebellion and unrest of the 1600s, the eighteenth century ushered in an era of greater political stability. However, successive land settlements during the seventeenth century had allowed a minority Protestant land-owning class to gain influence and control. Thus, while the vast majority (c. 90%) of the population of the county was Catholic, it held only one-sixth of the land. In fact, of the major ancient Irish families who held lands before the arrival of the Anglo-Normans in 1169, only the O'Conor Don retained them following the upheavals of the seventeenth century. The authority of the Protestant Ascendancy was copper-fastened by the introduction of the Penal Laws from 1695 onwards, which severely restricted the rights of Catholics. The dominance of agriculture in the economy increased even further the control, as well as the income, of the land-owning class.

The comparative peace allowed the Ascendancy to develop its estates and, in particular, to build fine residences which no longer needed to be fortified. One of the earliest surviving substantial houses is the King House in Boyle which dates from 1720-30 *(fig. 12)*. The King family was one of the most significant land-owning families in the county, holding almost thirty thousand acres. The land had been acquired in 1604 by Sir John King from Yorkshire, who was granted the lands of the dissolved Boyle Abbey by King James I. It was built by Sir Henry King, MP and third Baronet. It is unusual in being an estate house situated in a town. This is partly due to the fact that the house was built on the site of an earlier family home (c. 1650) which had been destroyed by fire in 1720.

The house is built on a grand scale; it is two storeys over basement, with a gabled attic, built

*(fig. 12)*
**KING HOUSE**
Main Street
Boyle
(1720)

This substantial house with its impressive skyline is one of the most important structures in Connacht. The well-proportioned façade with its Palladian detailing and finely executed stonework is attributed to the architect William Halfpenny, who built the house for Sir Henry King, who died in 1739. Though built in the Palladian style, this fine house retains a seventeenth-century fortified character, which must have served it well when it was used as a military barracks during the nineteenth and early-twentieth centuries.

*Courtesy of the National Library of Ireland.*

MILITARY BARRACK. BOYLE. 7371. W.L.

Ballymun Branch. Tel. 8421890

*(fig. 13)*
KING HOUSE
Main Street
Boyle

The plan is U-shaped and
consists of a main block
of north-south orientation
with two projecting pavilions to the north.

*(fig. 14)*
KING HOUSE
Main Street
Boyle

View of the tripartite
Venetian window on
each of the storeys.

on a U-shaped plan *(fig. 13)*. The architect is uncertain: it has been attributed to William Halfpenny (d. 1755), an assistant of Sir Edward Lovett Pearce, or Richard Castle (c. 1690-1751). It is architecturally impressive, and finished to an exceptionally high standard. All four levels are vaulted-over - an unusual and expensive feature. According to the Reverend Daniel Beaufort (1739-1821), the Church of Ireland minister and topographer, who was a visitor in 1787, this was a precaution against fire following the burning of the earlier house. In the side elevation of the house there is a tripartite Venetian window superimposed on each of the four storeys *(fig. 14)*. The ground floor is dominated by the Long Gallery which runs the full length of the building, each end terminated by a Venetian window.

The house seems not to have been completed as originally intended. Structural evidence has been found to suggest that the 'U' of the entrance front was intended to be built over, forming inside on the ground floor a grand entrance hall opening onto the Long Gallery. This possibly explains the lack of windows and somewhat 'blind' appearance of the entrance front today. After many years of neglect, the King House has recently undergone a magnificent restoration and it is now a civic amenity.

As Boyle grew during the eighteenth century, the geographical orientation of the King House in relation to the town changed. The house was originally set apart from the main axis of the town, which was north-south along the old road from Sligo (now Green Street), down the hill to the river and leaving the town along the road to Elphin. It is likely that, as the town grew, the pathway leading to the King House from the centre of the town became built up and eventually formed Main Street. Isaac Weld, in his Statistical Survey of the County of Roscommon (1832), criticised the way the house backs on to the river, setting the example for the later houses along Main Street, and wasting a great scenic potential. This was a result of the later evolution of the town, and subsequent to the building of the house. The house was originally situated in a larger demesne, with the river running through the garden to the rear.

The other surviving great house of the eighteenth century is Strokestown Park *(fig. 15)*. Like the King House in Boyle, it too was significant in the growth of the town in which it was built - but in a much more direct way. As has already been mentioned, the town was formally conceived by Maurice Mahon, and orientated on his demesne house, the vista along the grand main street of the town being terminated by the entrance gates of the house.

The estate originally belonged to the O'Conor Roe, but was acquired by the Mahon family in the seventeenth century. Nicholas Mahon (d. 1680), a military man, was granted a large portion of land for a deer park in 1653.

*(fig. 15)*
STROKESTOWN PARK
Bawn Street
Strokestown
(c. 1730)

Following the death of Sir Edward Lovett Pearce, his assistant German-born Richard Castle became one of Ireland's most celebrated architects. Castle went on to build some of the country's finest houses and is credited with much of the work at Strokestown Park. The elegant portico added in the nineteenth century provides a sense of grandeur.

*(fig. 16)*
**Stables**
**Strokestown Park**
**(c. 1730)**

The Italianate vaulted
stables, borne by a row
of Doric columns, were
in their day known as an
'equine cathedral'.

*(fig. 17)*
**Kitchen**
**Strokestown Park**

The left-hand pavilion
houses a rare surviving
example of a galleried
kitchen. From here the
mistress of Strokestown
or the housekeeper could
survey proceedings in
the kitchen below.

After the restoration of the monarchy in England, Nicholas pledged allegiance to Charles II and, in return for his loyalty, received a further grant of land. Nicholas commenced building a demesne house which was completed, after his death, in 1696. This house was then radically restructured and extended by Thomas Mahon (1701-82) in the 1730s, probably following his marriage in 1735. Remains of the older Mahon house still survive; the still-room in the basement of the current house has a Jacobean fireplace with heavy plaster decoration of swags and fruits, which suggests that this space was originally the dining room. At the same time as he was rebuilding the house, Thomas Mahon also carried out significant improvements to the estate lands. As well as improving the farmland, he established extensive plantations of trees. Arthur Young (1741-1820), the English agriculturalist, described the Strokestown woods in his Tour in Ireland (1776) as 'the finest woods I ever saw', being very extensive and 'of a great growth'.

The design of the eighteenth-century house has been ascribed to Richard Castle. The house is built in the Palladian style, composed of a seven-bay, three-storey central block, with two-storey wings that are joined to the main block by curved curtain walls. The niches in the latter, flanked by oculi above a blocked Gibbsian doorcase, are a characteristic feature of Castle's work. The wings contain the stables and the kitchen, which survive almost intact. The stables have beautiful plaster groin vaults supported by an elegant colonnade and they are similar to the stables at Carton and Russborough, both designed by Castle *(fig. 16)*. The galleried kitchen is probably the finest remaining example of its type in the country *(fig. 17)*. It is dominated by a row of ovens and ranges which spans the length of the room.

(fig. 18)
Entrance Gate
Strokestown Park
(c. 1790)

The comprehensive replanning of Strokestown is captured in the use of linear street plans with architecturally important buildings being treated as visual foci and procession-al axial vistas. This is emphasised by the length and width of the main street, which focuses on the gates and gate lodge of Strokestown Park at the east end, and termi-nates with St John's Church of Ireland at the west end.

Thomas Mahon was succeeded by his son Maurice (1738-1819) in 1782. Following the Act of Union in 1800, Maurice acquired a seat in the House of Lords and was created first Baron Hartland. He soon set about another phase of improvements to the estate. The grand picturesque Gothic gate which presents the house to the town was built in the 1790s *(fig. 18)*. The house underwent further alter-ations in the early nineteenth century. The façade of the eighteenth-century main block was remodelled. A Venetian window (in the central bay of the first floor) was removed, replaced by an ordinary sash, and a Regency Ionic portico was added. A tunnel was built to link the offices on either side of the house, so that the family did not have to see the staff go about their duties. Inside, a grand library was added and other reception rooms were redeco-rated *(fig. 19)*.

While the estate house of Strokestown dates mainly from the eighteenth century, the town was not really developed until the nineteenth, when Baron Hartland set about 'improving' the existing village. It was laid out between 1810 and 1815 on a grand scale. At nearly one hun-dred and fifty feet wide, the main thorough-fare, leading to the gates of the house, was said to have been the widest in Europe at the time. This formal plan was completed in 1819 with the building of a new Protestant church, St John's, at the opposite end of the main street, on axis with the house.

*(fig. 19)*
Reception Room
Strokestown Park

*(fig. 20)*
Walled Garden
Strokestown Park
Demesne
(c. 1730)

Ornamental walled garden, laid out c. 1730, with walled vegetable garden to south and mausoleum to west. These ornamental walled gardens and vegetable gardens have been returned to their former glory and are a beautifully maintained reminder of the estate's history.

Strokestown Park survives today remarkably unchanged since the alterations of the nineteenth century. It is valuable not only in its architectural fabric but more particularly for the insight it provides into eighteenth and nineteenth-century life. The house and gardens (which have been recently restored) are open to the public, along with the Famine Museum in the stable yards *(fig. 20)*. Strokestown was infamous during the Famine, both for the terrible suffering of its tenants and also for the assassination of its landlord, Major Denis Mahon (1787-1847). The extensive Strokestown estate papers are one of the most important such collections in the country and have been used to explain the significance of the Famine in national terms.

Sadly, the King House and Strokestown Park are the only two great houses of the eighteenth century still to survive in Roscommon. Many others have disappeared, including Mantua (c. 1747) and French Park (c. 1730) *(fig. 21)*, the designs of both have also been connected with Richard Castle. French Park was in a Palladian style similar to Strokestown Park; the interior was dismantled in the 1950s, and the ruin was finally demolished some years later. One of the few remaining demesne buildings of French Park is the smokehouse *(figs. 22-23)*. This unusual building, now derelict, is a rare survival and an important example of the variety of activities which took place on these demesnes. Another house which has disappeared is Mote Park, built in the late eigh-

*(fig. 21)*
**FRENCHPARK HOUSE**
**Frenchpark**
**(c. 1730)**

Frenchpark House was a three-storey house built for John French c. 1730 and probably to the design of Richard Castle. Following the standard Palladian layout, the two-storey pavilions were joined to the main block by plain curved sweeps. The interior was dismantled in the 1950s and the ruin demolished c. 1970.

*(fig. 22)*
Smokehouse
Frenchpark Demesne
(c. 1730)

*(fig. 23)*
**Smokehouse**
**Frenchpark Demesne**

The remains of the full-height central flue and hearth within the brick-lined interior with brick vaulted roof.

*(fig. 24)*
**MOTE PARK**
Ballymurray

Once the demesne of the Croftons, Mote Park was originally a late eigh-teenth-century irregular two-storey over basement house. The architect Richard Morrison more than doubled the size of the building by adding six bays and an extra storey. The house was destroyed by fire in 1865 and rebuilt with minor alterations. This photo-graph shows the entrance front following the alter-ations of 1865. The house was demolished c. 1958.

*Courtesy of the National Library of Ireland.*

*(fig. 25)*
**Entrance Gate**
**Mote Park Demesne**
**(c. 1800)**

Perhaps the most splendid surviving feature of Mote Park demesne is the origi-nal entrance gate. A Doric triumphal arch surmount-ed by a lion with screen walls link it to a pair of identical lodges.

*(fig. 26)*
**Entrance Gate**
**Mote Park Demesne**

*(fig. 27)*
**Entrance Gate**
**Mote Park Demesne**

teenth century but extensively altered in the early nineteenth by the architect, Richard Morrison (1767-1849) *(fig. 24)*. The gates of this substantial house are still extant, and are considered amongst the finest in the country. They are composed of a magnificent Doric triumphal arch surmounted by a lion, with screen walls linking them to a pair of lodges *(figs. 25-27)*. Similarities have been noted between these gates and those designed by James Gandon (1743-1823) at Carrigglas, County Longford.

In County Roscommon, the rate of survival of houses of the 'middle size' has been somewhat better than that of the large demesne houses. The Palladian style, so popular and effective in the larger houses around the country, was appropriated by builders of more modest sized houses. An early example was built in 1753 by Henry Fry at Boyle *(fig. 28)*. Fry established a weaving industry in the town and built a handsome house, Frybrook, in a picturesque setting, on the north bank of the river. It is a detached, five-bay, three-storey house with a hipped roof. The Palladian influence can be seen in the classical proportions, but more particularly in motifs such as the window scheme in the centre of the first floor elevation. The tripartite composition with a round-headed central window is a simplified version of what is known as a serliana, or Palladian window. The pedimented entrance and the oculus (round window) in the centre of the top storey are also motifs derived from Palladian classicism. A distinctive feature, curious for the time and for the scale of the house, is that Frybrook lacks a basement.

Scregg, near Knockcroghery in the south of the county, was built a little later, c. 1765 *(fig. 29)*. It also reflects the local influence of

*(fig. 28)*
**FRYBROOK HOUSE**
**Boyle**
**(1753)**

Although Frybrook appears quite plain, it exhibits some delicate classical detailing such as the Venetian window, the pedimented entrance, the oculus and the proportions of the overall house. A notable feature of this house is the absence of a basement which is very unusual for a house of this size and date.

Palladianism, this time in a rural setting. It is a house of five bays and three storeys over a basement and is gable-ended with a pitched roof. Scregg has a Palladian window similar to Frybrook's, but it also has a Diocletian window (a tripartite segmental scheme) in the centre of the top storey - another feature popular in Palladianism. The façade is further enlivened by the rusticated window surrounds and the tripartite doorway with its idiosyncratic reference to classical architecture, the columns standing proud of the entablature *(fig. 30)*. Another feature of interest can be found in the coach-house to the west of the main house. Replacement copies of two sheela-na-gigs, ancient female exhibitionist figures carved in stone, are inserted in the gable wall. Scregg is a valuable example of an eighteenth-century country house, of fine architectural quality, which has survived without alteration.

*(fig. 29)*
**SCREGG HOUSE**
**Knockcroghery**
**(c. 1765)**

This five-bay three-storey over basement house, with rusticated surrounds to the windows and quoins, has a pedimented and columned Georgian doorcase.

*(fig. 30)*
**SCREGG HOUSE**
**Knockcroghery**

Tripartite doorway at Scregg with columns standing proud of the entablature.

*(fig. 31)*
**BUSHYPARK HOUSE**
Mount Talbot
(c. 1720)

The well-proportioned front elevation of Bushypark House exhibits the symmetry characteristic of early Irish Georgian architecture. The orderly composition of the front elevation fenestration is relieved by the octagonal window to the attic storey. Used formerly as a school for the sons of Protestant clergymen and the home of the ffrench family, Bushypark House has played a significant role in the social history of Mount Talbot and its environs.

*(fig. 32)*
**SCARTOWN HOUSE**
Castlecoote
(c. 1700)

Scartown House, reached by a long driveway, was originally built as a 'long house' with rooms opening directly into one another and access by a single entry-passage. The farmhouse was later altered, taking on the form seen today.

Bushypark House, near Mount Talbot, is a smaller and earlier example of a country house *(fig. 31)*. Built c. 1720, it is of five bays with a gable-ended pitched roof - thus broadly similar to Scregg. However, it is one storey lower and has none of the Palladian classical detailing of the later house. The only decoration is the simple block-and-start surround of the round-headed door opening; nevertheless its symmetry and proportions create a fine composition.

An interesting example of what was originally an eighteenth-century traditional vernacular house is Scartown House in Castlecoote *(fig. 32)*. Dating from c. 1700, it has undergone some alteration since it was originally built, yet it still retains its early character. Castle Coote House has already been mentioned as having pre-1700 origins. Built in the early seventeenth century, the original star-fort was radically rebuilt in a classical style, c. 1770. Two of the original flanking towers were incorporated into the main house to the north and south; full

height bows were added to the south and west elevations. In fact, the house, as it appears today, shows little evidence of its pre-1700 fortified origins. Various remnants of the original buildings, such as the stable complex, can be found around the grounds of the house.

From the mid-1730s there followed a period of sustained economic growth in Ireland. The expansion in the agricultural sector led to rising prices and a growth in trade. This increase in agricultural productivity lead to a commensurate growth in related industrial development throughout the country. While farming in Roscommon was dominated by sheep-rearing, evidence remains of the growth of industries such as milling.

In Castlerea, a corn-mill was built in the early years of the century by the local landlords, the Sandfords of Castlereagh House (now demolished) *(fig. 33)*. The buildings are now derelict, but it is still possible to see that it comprised a complex of four abutting buildings. The remains survive of the mill-wheel and race, and the workers' accommodation. The mill would have been significant in the development of Castlerea, settlement beginning originally at this end of the town and growing eastwards. According to Samuel Lewis in his Topographical Dictionary of Ireland (1837), there was at that date a 'very extensive distillery' (which was connected with the corn-mill, along with a brewery and tannery), producing

*(fig. 33)*
Corn Mill
Castlerea
(c. 1725)

This mill complex, originally built by the Sandfords of Castlereagh House, comprises an interesting group of mill-related structures including an intact mill wheel, mill race and mill workers' accommodation to the east of the site.

more than 20,000 gallons of whiskey annually. Even in its sad state today, the derelict mill is an evocative and important reminder of the town's industrial past.

Another mill complex, dating from the end of the century, survives in Athleague *(fig. 34)*. This mill is also no longer in use, but it is more intact than the one in Castlerea. In addition to the four-storey mill building, there is an operating mill-wheel and race *(fig. 35)*, as well as a drying-kiln. The adjacent weir and sluice provide a dramatic illustration of the industrial practices involved in the milling process. The good network of rivers meant that mills were also established in other places around the county, such as in Roosky, Lecarrow and Boyle.

*(fig. 34)*
Water Mill
Athleague
(c. 1800)

The mill, kiln and ancillary structures form an interesting group of industrial buildings with the adjacent weir and sluice.

*(fig. 35)*
Water Mill
Athleague

Detail of mill wheel.

Windmills were erected in a number of places, the open expanses of parts of the county being very suitable. They were mostly erected by local landlords who obliged their tenants to mill their grain there and pay a toll for the privilege. A rare insight into this aspect of Ireland's industrial heritage can be found at the fine windmill in Elphin *(fig. 36)*. The windmill was originally built about 1730, probably by the local land-owner, the Bishop of Elphin, Edward Synge. After the Napoleonic wars ended in 1815, cereal-milling became less profitable and many windmills fell into disuse thereafter; that at Elphin was already in ruins by the 1830s. It was restored to full working order and was opened as a visitor attraction in 1996. It is a round three-stage structure with a rye-thatch rotating roof and has four timber sails.

The ruins of a few other windmill structures survive. One such example is the Loobinroe Windmill, at Correal, near Mount Talbot, which was built about 1750 *(figs. 37-38)*. Like the windmill at Elphin, it is a three-stage structure, but the battered, or sloping, walls of random-coursed rubble-stone masonry give it a more imposing presence. Sited in an elevated position and enclosed by a stone wall, it remains, though ruined, an impressive structure.

*(fig. 36)*
**ELPHIN WINDMILL**
Windmill Road
Elphin
(c. 1730)

This early-eighteenth century fully restored windmill is a credit to the town of Elphin. It stands as a reminder of when the mill, thought to have been originally built by local landowner and Bishop of Elphin, Edward Synge, provided meal for the local population. By 1830 the mill was in ruins. It was sympathetically restored under a three-year project by a FÁS social employment scheme.

(fig. 37)
**LOOBINROE WINDMILL**
**Mount Talbot**
(c. 1750)

Located on an elevated site, the structure has commanding views of the surrounding countryside.

(fig. 38)
**LOOBINROE WINDMILL**
**Mount Talbot**

*(fig. 39)*
**BANK OF IRELAND**
**The Square**
**Roscommon**
**(1750)**

Originally built as a rectangular-plan courthouse in the mid-eighteenth century, this building, having become derelict, was bought by the Parish Priest Fr John Madden in 1829, at the time of Catholic Emancipation and converted into a Roman Catholic church. The front and rear additions were erected in 1844. The finely executed stone of the façade is embellished by the pediments and carved stone dressings such as the Ionic pilasters below the cupola.

*(fig. 40)*
**ROSCOMMON LIBRARY**
**Abbey Town**
**Roscommon**
**(1783)**

This impressive public building, once used as an infirmary, was built by Mrs. Walcott, sister of Lord Chief Justice Caulfield in 1783 to house the poor of the county. It stands as a prominent edifice with the eighteenth-century central block, nineteenth-century large tower and flanking wings out-scaling the surrounding buildings. Its balanced and symmetrical design is enlivened by elaborate fenestration and dressed stonework.

Following the Anglo-Norman invasion in 1169, a new administrative system was imposed on the country: the Grand Jury became the primary means of local government. The members of the Grand Jury were selected from the leading male property-owners of each county. Its responsibilities included the supervision of the law, as well as the funding of road- and bridge-building and maintenance. In the eighteenth century its powers were extended to include the building and repair of gaols and courthouses, as well as the establishment of county infirmaries. A fine example of each of these building types can be found in Market Square in Roscommon town.

The Old Gaol, of c. 1740, is an imposing building which still dominates the centre of the town. It is attributed locally to Richard Castle. Although now much altered internally, the front façade has been retained. The castellated parapet and fortified appearance of the corner towers, as well as its prominent position, would have been an intimidating reminder of the authority of the law over the town. However, it served as a gaol for less than a century, being superseded by the building of a new complex in 1814, to the designs of Richard Morrison; this later building was demolished c. 1945. The Old Gaol has fulfilled a variety of functions over the years; it served as an asylum, a refuge, a market house and a private house. It is now a commercial premises combined with residential accommodation.

Facing the Old Gaol, across the square, is the former courthouse, now the Bank of Ireland *(fig. 39)*. Built c. 1765, it too is an imposing building, this time in the classical style. In 1762, the Grand Jury commissioned George Ensor, a Dublin architect, to build a new session and market house on the site of the old session house. The contract price was £1,200. When a new courthouse was built in 1822, the building was purchased by the parish priest on behalf of the townspeople. It became the Roman Catholic parish church of Roscommon town in 1836.

The two-storey building is cruciform in plan with a hipped slate roof. The pedimented porch and the tower with copper cupola seem to have been added when the courthouse was converted to a church. The orientation of the building also probably changed at this time; it seems that it originally fronted onto the square, facing the Old Gaol. The building is highly finished, with ashlar masonry on the front and rear elevations. It is a fully classical building, both in its proportions and in its use of the classical orders: for example, the pilasters supporting the entablature of the front porch.

The county infirmary of Roscommon was built in 1783, in Abbeytown, to the south of the town centre *(fig. 40)*. It was apparently built at the sole expense of a Mrs Walcott, sister of the Lord Chief Justice Caulfield. It contained over fifty beds, and had a small detached fever hospital as well as a dispensary for the treatment of out-patients. The building comprises a three bay, three-storey over basement central block, with flanking wings. The building was considerably altered in the nineteenth century; the tower and wings that now exist were not part of the original structure. The infirmary was renovated in 1928-29, but it closed in 1941. It re-opened in 1948 as Roscommon County Library headquarters and branch library.

While the building of gaols, courthouses and infirmaries was generally funded by the Grand Juries, another example of public architecture - places of worship - was not. The political unrest of the sixteenth and seventeenth centuries had largely precluded the building of churches. Even the greater stability of the eighteenth century did not immediately usher in a new era of church-building.

The Penal Laws had placed restrictions on Roman Catholic worship, and hence on the building of churches. Nevertheless, a remarkable penal chapel survives near Ballaghaderreen. The Four Altars, of about 1750, is a cruciform chapel, with open niches to the arms and a stone cross on the roof *(fig. 41)*. It is built of random-coursed limestone and has a corbelled stone roof. The perfect simplicity of its plan makes it an evocative reminder of the penal times. Its prominent location, on an elevated site, seems curious in the context of the time.

The Catholic graveyard at Keadew was established, around 1755, on the site of a fourteenth-century church, the remains of which are still standing. Within the walls of the ruined church lies the grave of Turlough O'Carolan, the celebrated blind harpist and 'the last of the Irish bards', who died in 1738 at Alderford in Ballyfarnan *(fig. 42)*. The graveyard was repaired and enlarged in 1858, at which time the sandstone entrance arch was erected by Lady Louisa Tenison.

For the Established Church (the Church of Ireland), the Board of First Fruits was established in 1711 to fund the building and repair of churches and glebe houses. However, a significant increase in rural church-building did not really take place until the nineteenth century. Nevertheless, there were a few new

*(fig. 42)*
Roman Catholic
Cemetery
Keadew

The gateway, erected by Lady Louisa Tenison in 1858, bears this inscription in the tympanum: Within this churchyard lies interred Carolan, the last of the Irish Bards. He died March 25th 1738. R.I.P.

*(fig. 41)*
THE FOUR ALTARS
Ballaghaderreen
(c. 1750)

The particular religious landmark highlights the importance of Christian symbolism in rural Ireland.

(fig. 43)
**KILRONAN CHURCH OF
IRELAND CHURCH**
Keadew
(c. 1790)

Although situated on an elevated site, the church is screened from the road and neighbouring houses by mature trees, thus presenting an appealing vista on entering the gates.

churches built towards the very end of the century. The classical church at Boyle erected c. 1790 is a fine example, built on an elevated site to the north of the town. It has an unusual, truncated cruciform plan; effectively a T-plan extended by a curved chancel. It is a striking building from the exterior. The west front is an imposing façade which combines restrained classicism with an impressive castellated tower.

At Kilronan, the Church of Ireland church, of a similar date to Boyle, is much closer to what would become the typical Board of First Fruits type in the nineteenth century *(fig. 43)*. A simple three-bay nave with diamond-tracery lancet windows, it has a projecting gable to the east and a castellated tower forming the west front. The poorer quality of the stone in the tower and west gable suggests they might originally have been rendered. Like many Church of Ireland churches around the country, it is now no longer in use and is a vulnerable part of the county's architectural heritage *(fig. 44)*.

(fig. 44)
**KILRONAN CHURCH OF
IRELAND CHURCH**
Keadew

# The Nineteenth Century

The nineteenth century introduced a period of rapid social and political change, along with an increase in population. The Act of Union came into effect on 1 January 1801, after which time the main political issues were repeal of the Act and the campaign for Catholic Emancipation. The latter was finally achieved in 1829, but repeal was a much more difficult issue and the struggle for Home Rule continued throughout the century. Tensions had been already growing within Irish society from the late 1770s. The American War of Independence fomented unrest around Ireland and ultimately brought about the granting of free trade in 1779, and so-called legislative independence in 1782. In the 1790s the French Revolution and the subsequent wars between England and France added to the political instability of the period.

While events in America had an impact on the economy and politics of Ireland, the war with France was a much more immediate threat to the ruling authorities. The attempted French invasion at Bantry Bay of 1796 and the events of 1798, culminating in the French landing at Killala, showed the vulnerability of the country to the very real threat of invasion. The importance of defending the coast was keenly felt. To this end, when hostilities broke out again against France in 1803, a major building programme of defensive works was instigated. Over fifty martello towers were built around the coast, along with batteries and signal towers.

The French force which had landed at Killala in 1798 had succeeded in crossing the Shannon, highlighting the importance of defending the crossing-points of the river. Perhaps the most impressive structure to be built was the massive bridgehead (or tête-de-pont) defence at Shannonbridge (1812-17) *(figs. 45-46)*. It was built to defend the highly strategic and immense masonry bridge, completed in 1757 *(fig. 47)*. The structure has sixteen arches (an additional navigation arch was added in the nineteenth century) and was very significant in the internal communications of the country generally. In the early nineteenth century it was the nearest crossing-point of the river to Galway Bay.

The Shannonbridge fortifications are laid out on the west bank of the river, on high ground, in an almost symmetrical arrangement, in line with the axis of the bridge. The complex was built on a triangular plan with corner bastions. It comprises a front glacis (a steep slope), behind which is an armed redoubt with gun-loop openings. Projecting into the ditch separating the glacis and redoubt is a caponnière, a bomb-proof vaulted structure, with musket-loops flanking the ditch. Behind these defensive structures, closest to the bridge, is a barracks and a small-arms battery. The barracks is a massive twelve-bay, three-storey building, with strongly battered walls *(fig. 48)*. The building itself was defensible: the roof is flat, supported by barrel vaults below, and it

*(fig. 45)*
SHANNONBRIDGE TÊTE-DE-PONT
Shannonbridge
(1810-1817)

The construction of the present extensive masonry fortification on the west bank to replace the two earthwork redoubts possibly started in 1811-12, when it appears that the fieldworks along the Shannon began to be superseded by permanent defences. The fortifications are laid out in an almost symmetrical arrangement on the axis of the bridge.

*Courtesy of Simmons Aerofilms Limited.*

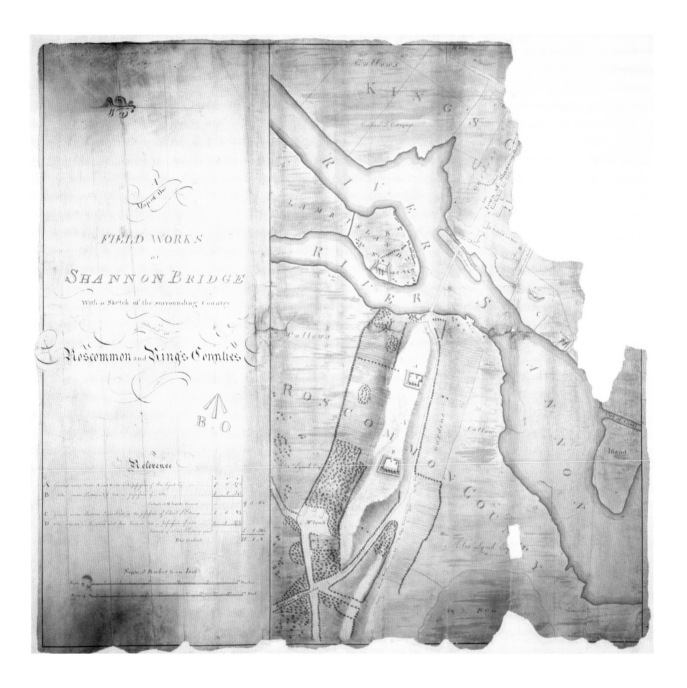

**(fig. 46)**
**'A Map of the FIELD WORKS at SHANNON BRIDGE With a Sketch of the surrounding Country Situated in Roscommon and King's Counties'**
**(1810)**

Drawn to a scale of around 170 feet to one inch, this map shows the field works, i.e. defensive works, at Shannonbridge located on the River Shannon between counties Roscommon and Offaly (formerly King's County). The map shows redoubts A and B and batteries Nos 1, 2 and 3. Shannonbridge, as the name implies, was one of the few locations where the river could be crossed. The bridge illustrated in the map still stands today.

*Courtesy of the National Archives, Kew, Surrey, United Kingdom.*

**(fig. 47)**
**SHANNONBRIDGE**
**(1757)**

This bridge spans the River Shannon, which marks the boundary of the provinces of Connacht and Leinster.

*(fig. 48)*
**SHANNONBRIDGE TÊTE-DE-PONT**

East elevation of left (southern) flank barrack. The flat-roofed gun platform is carried on barrel vaulting.

*(fig. 49)*
**SHANNONBRIDGE TÊTE-DE-PONT**

The walls are blank, except for the cut stone musket loops, and slope inwards with a pronounced batter.

had three guns on traversing platforms. It has been noted that the barracks presents a domestic appearance towards the east but a very warlike aspect to the west *(fig. 49)*. Altogether, this complex of buildings is unique in Ireland or Britain, and has been described as a 'remarkable example of artillery fortification of the Napoleonic period'.

The early decades of the nineteenth century saw an improvement in communications through the country - both river and road. Along the River Shannon the first major campaign of navigation improvements (between Killaloe and Carrick-on-Shannon) had been completed between 1755 and circa 1769. The second campaign (of similar geographical extent) was between 1839-50. With the Shannon forming most of the eastern boundary of Roscommon, these improvements had a strong impact on communications within the county.

The five-arch road-bridge at Roosky on the county boundary with Leitrim is an example of the Shannon Navigation Commissioners' second campaign of improvements *(fig. 50)*. Built in 1845, it is typical of the design adopted by their engineer, Thomas Rhodes. The low segmental profile of the arches makes it possible to maintain a level roadway for the full width of the bridge. With the adjacent moorings and quay, the bridge would have been an important factor in the growth of the settlement. As improvements continued to be made to the river during the century, ancillary structures, such as the stepped cut-stone beacon, were erected *(fig. 51)*. Although simply fulfilling a navigational function, the beacon is attractively composed and has well-executed stonework.

*(fig. 50)*
ROOSKY BRIDGE
(1845)

*(fig. 51)*
Beacon
Roosky
(c. 1880)

This beacon forms part of an interesting and significant group of structures with the bridge, quay and mooring posts.

(fig. 52)
**BALLYFORAN BRIDGE**
**Ballyforan**
**(c. 1820)**

Ballyforan Bridge is a substantial road bridge, which forms an important crossing point between Counties Galway and Roscommon.

(fig. 53)
**BOYLE BRIDGE**
**Bridge Street**
**Boyle**
**(1864)**

In 1837 Samuel Lewis described this bridge as a 'handsome structure of three arches, 100 feet long and 42 feet wide...the lightness and beauty of the design add greatly to the appearance of the town...'

*Courtesy of the National Library of Ireland.*

(fig. 54)
Benchmark
Ballaghaderreen
(c. 1830)

Benchmarks are an
attractive and subtle item
of street furniture. Of
considerable historical
importance, they attest to
the work of the Ordnance
Survey in mapping all of
Ireland in the nineteenth
century.

Of course, improvements also took place on other rivers around the county during the nineteenth century: for example, the impressive thirteen-arch road-bridge over the River Suck at Ballyforan, on the border with Galway *(fig. 52)*. Built about 1820, the long bridge is constructed of random-coursed stone walls with cut-limestone voussoirs to the arches, and V-shaped cutwaters to both the up- and downstream sides. The great length of the bridge conveys the scale of the engineering improvements which took place during the early years of the century.

The early decades of the century also saw an improvement in the county's road network. In Roscommon the evolution of roads had been a slow process. By the time of Weld's Statistical Survey of 1832 there were just two mail-coach roads (first-rate roads) running through the county in a broadly east-west direction, with a third in progress. The two older routes were to the far north and south of the county: crossing from Carrick-on-Shannon to Boyle, on the way to Sligo, and from Athlone towards Ballinasloe, on the way to Galway. The third route crossed the county via Strokestown. In the same survey, the author described how the general improvement of roads had been 'very remarkable' in the twenty years before 1832, and that markets and towns had increased as a consequence.

A significant part of the process of improving communications within the county was the work of the Ordnance Survey. Although it was established in 1824 with the aim of calculating the acreage of townlands as an aid to standardising local taxation, the mapping work would have been essential to the improvement of the road and river navigation network. A remnant of the work of the Ordnance Survey can be found in the pair of limestone 'crow's foot' benchmarks in Ballaghaderreen *(fig. 54)*.

*(fig. 55)*
**ROSCOMMON RAILWAY STATION**
(c. 1860)

Roscommon Railway Station was built by the Midland Great Western Railway Company. The attractive gable treatment, decorative canopy and tooled stone dressings add artistic interest to the building.

*(fig. 56)*
**Waiting Room**
**ROSCOMMON RAILWAY STATION**

This structure forms part of an architecturally interesting group of buildings at Roscommon Railway Station.

The advent of the railway in Roscommon, from 1860, linked the county into a wider, national network. As was common in this era of railway-building, the stations were well-executed architectural statements. While the great railway termini of Dublin were designed as monumental buildings in a classical mode, the many small stations around the country were designed in a wide variety of architectural styles. The station at Roscommon town, in an Elizabethan style, is a particularly fine example *(fig. 55)*. It is a seven-bay, single-storey build-ing, with a projecting gable-fronted entrance porch. There is a liveliness about the architectural details: the tall ornate chimneys and the raised curvilinear gable ends with finials. The station is faced in cut stone and finished to a high degree, with fine tooled-stone dressings. The related buildings and structures are also important parts of the station complex: for example, the single-storey waiting room *(fig. 56)*, of timber panelling and stone, and the cast-iron footbridge.

*(fig. 57)*
Signal Cabin
ROSCOMMON RAILWAY
STATION

*(fig. 58)*
ROSCOMMON RAILWAY
STATION

Detail of signal.

The station at Carrick-on-Shannon is simpler and more classical in style *(fig. 59)*. The random-coursed limestone of its front and rear elevations contrasts with the tooled limestone quoins and window surrounds. The segmental-headed window openings add a character to the elevation, which might otherwise be somewhat austere. The station was built to the designs of George Wilkinson (1814-90) who, as architect to the Poor Law Board and the Board of Control for Lunatic Asylums, is better known as the designer of workhouses and asylums throughout Ireland. Wilkinson undertook commissions for a number of railway companies, but especially for the Midland Great Western Railway Company. He was also possibly the architect of Roscommon station. At Carrick-on-Shannon, as at Roscommon, there is a fine collection of ancillary station buildings and structures, such as the former waiting room, with timber panelled walls and decorative bracing below the windows *(fig. 60)*. Another fine structure is the footbridge with beautifully detailed cast-iron foliate panels *(figs. 61-62)*.

*(fig. 59)*
CARRICK-ON-SHANNON
RAILWAY STATION

*(fig. 60)*
Waiting Room
CARRICK-ON-SHANNON
RAILWAY STATION

*(fig. 62)*
Footbridge
CARRICK-ON-SHANNON
RAILWAY STATION

Detail of the cast-iron
foliate panels at the
parapet.

*(fig. 61)*
Footbridge
CARRICK-ON-SHANNON
RAILWAY STATION

*(fig. 63)*
**ARIGNA RAILWAY STA-
TION**

This photo, which dates
from 1959, shows Arigna
Railway Station. A
tramway originally serv-
iced Arigna and operated
between 1836 and 1838.

*Courtesy of the National
Library of Ireland.*

*(fig. 64)*
Train crossing bridge near
Shannonbridge.

*Courtesy of the National
Library of Ireland.*

*(fig. 65)*
**ROCKINGHAM HOUSE**
Boyle
**(1810)**

This drawing shows John Nash's original design for Rockingham. Originally two storeys with a curved central bow fronted by a semicircular Ionic colonnade and surmounted by a dome. Although the main house was burnt down in 1957 and subsequently demolished, much of the ancillary demesne structures survive.

## PLAN OF THE GROUND STORY.

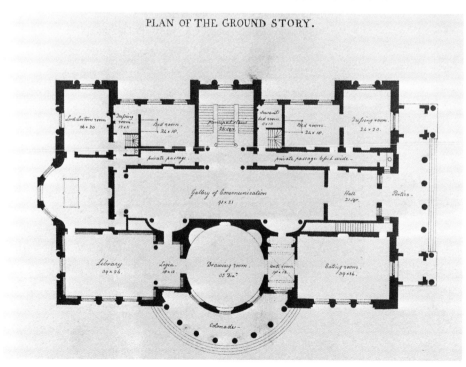

*(fig. 66)*
**ROCKINGHAM HOUSE**
Boyle
**(1810)**

Plan of the ground floor. Inspired by the classical villa, the house was made up by a series of alternating façades with no back entrance. The plan for Rockingham included the entrance in the short elevation and a suite of reception rooms, including a domed rotunda, on one long façade overlooking Lough Key.

The demesne house is an architectural type that, in Ireland, is very much associated with the eighteenth century. However, in County Roscommon the most magnificent example was built in the nineteenth century: Rockingham, on the shores of Lough Key, near Boyle. The house was built from 1810 by Robert Edward King, first Viscount Lorton (1773-1854), a descendant of Sir Henry King, who had built King House in Boyle. King House was sold to the army and converted into a barracks at the end of the eighteenth century. The family subsequently lived in a house at Rockingham, their lakeside demesne outside Boyle, and in their Dublin town house in Henrietta Street. However, in 1809 Viscount Lorton set about building a grand new house on the picturesque Rockingham demesne. John Nash (1752-1835), the English Picturesque architect, received the commission.

The house was set on an elevated site, with panoramic views of lakes and wooded park-land. The history of the building is complicated to trace because the original house underwent later alterations, was then badly damaged by fire in 1860 and rebuilt, before finally being demolished following another fire in 1957. Something of Nash's original design can be seen in an oil painting of 1818/19 of the Rockingham demesne, by James Arthur O'Connor. The house was an asymmetrical classical villa with a central domed tempietto and an entrance colonnade *(fig. 65)*. The entrance was in the short elevation of the house; this allowed a suite of reception rooms to run, uninterrupted, the length of the long façade, overlooking the lake *(fig. 66)*. The house was much altered in 1822 by the removal of the dome and the addition of a second storey, which spoilt the picturesque variety of Nash's original design. Something of the impact of these alterations can be seen in the photograph of the house of c. 1910 *(fig. 67)*.

Rockingham, Boyle.                    Co. Roscommon.

*(fig. 67)*
**ROCKINGHAM HOUSE**
Boyle
(c. 1910)

This photograph dating from c. 1910 shows the impact of the works of 1822 and 1863. In 1822 an extra storey was added, at the cost of sacrificing the dome. Either in 1822 or in c. 1863, following serious fire damage, the porch on the entrance front was replaced by the balustraded porte cochère. The recessed Ionic columns in the principal front were also removed.

*(fig. 68)*
Servants' Tunnels
Rockingham Demesne

All services to the house
were hidden underground
in elaborate tunnels that
linked the house to the
stable block, the icehouse
and the river.

*(fig. 69)*
Servants' Tunnels
Rockingham Demesne

While nothing of the house remains, a sense of the scale and grandeur of the entire scheme can be found in the surviving network of servants' tunnels like those already seen at Strokestown *(figs. 68-69)*. The remains also survive of the icehouse, which was an essential for the maintenance of an estate house of this scale *(figs. 70-71)*.

Following the fire in 1957, the Stafford-King-Harman family sold the estate to the Department of Lands, who, despite initial plans to restore the house, razed it to the ground in 1970. Nevertheless, a remarkable collection of ancillary estate buildings, such as gate-lodges, bridges, follies and a mock castle, remains in the demesne. Some of these, such as the picturesque estate church, now only survive as ruins. Others, such as the fine Gothic-style gate-lodge, though intact, are no longer in use and are therefore in a vulnerable state *(figs. 72-74)*. Also in poor condition is the range of fine stable buildings, which still retains many original features *(figs. 75-76)*.

*(fig. 70)*
Icehouse
**Rockingham Demesne**
**(c. 1810)**

The icehouse, which was situated on the shores of Lough Key, was an integral part of the estate architecture and lifestyle. It enabled the gentry to have the freshest of food delivered to their tables.

*(fig. 71)*
Icehouse
**Rockingham Demesne**

Detail of corbelled brick roof.

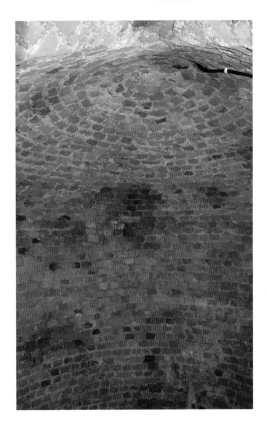

*(fig. 72)*
**Gate house**
**Rockingham Demesne**

This Gothic style gate house formed a spectacular entrance into Rockingham Demesne. It was possibly designed by the architect John Nash, who was responsible for the house, or by his draftsman Humphrey Repton, who is credited with the design of many of the lodges. With its crenellated parapet and Gothic style, it differs hugely from the other more classically designed lodges associated with the demesne.

*(fig. 73)*
**Gate house**
**Rockingham Demesne**

A notable feature of the fine stonework is the extensive use of punched limestone dressing. Without exception, all of the limestone dressing has been punch-dressed from plinth through to parapet, including the vaulted ceiling of the carriage arch and the bollards which line the roadway, protecting the gate house itself from damage by carriage wheels.

*(fig. 74)*
Gate house
Rockingham Demesne

*(fig. 75)*
**Stables**
**Rockingham Demesne**
**(1810; 1845)**

Built in at least two
phases, this stable com-
plex remains virtually
intact. The circular win-
dows, niches and vaulted
roof to the carriage arch
are particularly notewor-
thy features.

*(fig. 76)*
**Stables**
**Rockingham Demesne**
**(1810; 1845)**

The stables are enhanced
by the retention of many
original items such as the
cobbled and paved yard
with stone drain, where
the water pump was once
located, the sliding grid
like gates set on runners,
stable interiors and stairs
to former head and assis-
tant groomsmen quarters.

The variety and range of buildings around the demesne is astonishing. There is the remarkable bow-fronted and colonnaded 'tiara' gate-lodge *(fig. 77)*, which is fully classical and has extremely high-quality stonework *(figs. 78-79)*. There are picturesque hunting lodges in a romantic castellated style, such as Carty's Castle *(fig. 80)* and the now ruined Cloontykilla Castle *(figs. 81-83)*. The

*(fig. 77)*
**RATHDIVEEN LODGE**
**Rockingham Demesne**
**(1810)**

This classical colonnaded gate lodge was designed by John Nash or possibly by Nash's draftsman, Humphrey Repton. The classical gates, which give access into the former Rockingham Demesne, compliment the bowed façade.

*(fig. 78)*
**RATHDIVEEN LODGE**
**Rockingham Demesne**

The detail of the frieze on the gate piers is echoed in the frieze of the lodge.

*(fig. 79)*
**RATHDIVEEN LODGE**
**Rockingham Demesne**

These gates were recently moved to accommodate the widening of the main Dublin-Sligo road.

*(fig. 80)*
**CARTY'S CASTLE**
**Rockingham Demesne**
**(c. 1810)**

This former hunting lodge, situated on a height overlooking Lough Key, was in the past linked by canal to Lough Key. It is locally attributed to John Nash, although he may have only embellished an existing house. Despite the loss of some original features and a fifth tower, the remaining four castellated towers and rear elevation present an unusual and visually striking exterior.

*(fig. 81)*
**CLOONTYKILLA CASTLE**
**Rockingham Demesne**
**(1839)**

Cloontykilla Castle is located on the shores of Lough Key in a remote part of Cloontykilla Woods. Though derelict now, this castle was once a fanciful retreat for its owners. Its composition of crenellated walls, enclosing a yard and small house, is unusual and appealing. The impression of compact accommodation within the walls is deceptive and the castle was probably used as a hunting or fishing lodge. The crenellated and battered walls, towers and grid style gates romantically recall medieval castles.

*(fig. 82)*
**CLOONTYKILLA CASTLE**
Rockingham Demesne

*(fig. 83)*
**CLOONTYKILLA CASTLE**
Rockingham Demesne

Ballymun Branch. Tel. 8421890

*(fig. 86)*
**FISHING LODGE**
**ROCKINGHAM DEMESNE**
**(c. 1810)**

This gazebo functions
as a fishing house. It
also provides an ideal
spot from which to
admire Lough Key and
the folly castle on the
island opposite.

*(fig. 84)*
**FAIRY BRIDGE**
Rockingham Demesne
(1836)

Fairy Bridge is of a scale
and design that is excep-
tional in Ireland. It has a
considerable span, five
times the width of the
narrow canal which it
bridges. This canal links
two inlets of Lough Key.

*(fig. 85)*
**FAIRY BRIDGE**
Rockingham Demesne

The use of river-worn
limestone in its construction and its undulating
form give it a fairytale
and almost grotesque
quality.

landscaping of the demesne also included bridges and eye-catchers, such as the elaborate, wildly grotesque, rustic stone Fairy Bridge *(figs. 84-85)* or the circular fishing 'temple' or gazebo at the end of a causeway, projecting into the lake *(figs. 86-87)*. The landscaping of the demesne was carried out by a celebrated English landscape gardener, John Sutherland. Sutherland was also a competent builder, and it has been suggested that many of the demesne buildings might have been carried out to his designs.

Gate-lodges were built on estates of all sizes throughout the county. A fine example of c. 1820 is at Ballydooley, near Ballintober *(fig. 88)*. It is single storey, three bay, with a hipped roof and centrally placed chimney stacks. Although modest in scale, it is well proportioned and has fine architectural detailing, such as the simple classical doorcase. This classic lodge-type became a popular model for individual rural houses in the first half of the twentieth century.

*(fig. 87)*
**Boat Harbour**
**Rockingham Demesne**

The fishing lodge can be seen in the background.

*Courtesy of the National Library of Ireland.*

*(fig. 88)*
**Gate-Lodge**
**Ballydooley**
**(c. 1820)**

This modest lodge is small in scale yet articulates the symmetry and architectural detailing popular and fashionable at the time of its construction.

Although great improvements were carried out on their land by some of the landlords (in the form of improved agricultural practices, plantations and the building of towns, such as Strokestown), overall the improvements made upon estates did not impact on the greater population. As the horrific impact of the Great Famine (1845-50) took its toll, many of the landlords, being absentees, took little interest. However, some of those who were resident did their best to help. Lord de Freyne of French Park and Viscount Lorton of Rockingham donated money and established relief committees. Viscount Lorton made a plea to the House of Lords for help for Ireland. Lorton was an austere landlord, but was respected by many of his tenants, particularly due to his efforts during the famine years. Later in the century, Lorton's younger son, Laurence Harman King-Harman, inherited the estate. By this time it was ridden with debt. However, King-Harman set about improving the estate once more, and saved it from bankruptcy. He is commemorated by a clock tower in the Crescent in Boyle, which was erected around 1880, by subscription of his tenants *(fig. 89)*.

Following the Great Famine, the economy started to improve in the 1850s and 1860s. However, there was never again to be a building campaign of great houses as had been seen in the eighteenth century. Instead were built some substantial middle-sized houses. Carrowroe Park, of c. 1820, is an early example of this type. In its proportions and scale, the house is very much of the nineteenth century. The wings with pairs of pedimented pavilions were added in the early twentieth century *(fig. 90)*. The house is accompanied by a fine complex of stables and farmyard *(fig. 91)*.

*(fig. 89)*
BOYLE TOWN CLOCK
The Crescent
Boyle
(c. 1880)

*(fig. 90)*
**CARROWROE PARK**
**(c. 1820)**

Late Georgian villa with later Grecian wings (built 1907), one temple-like, the other containing the kitchen.

*(fig. 91)*
**Stables**
**Carrowroe Park**

The pedimented break-front motif as found on the main house is carried through to the coach houses. Two identical two-storey coach houses face each other across the yard and are linked by a single-storey stable block.

*(fig. 92)*
**EDMONDSTOWN HOUSE**
**(1864)**

Edmondstown House is a rare example of High Victorian Gothic in County Roscommon. It displays those features typical of High Victorian architecture, which include the octagonal tower, string courses of red brick framing the pointed-arched window openings and the decorative cast-iron roof finials.

*(fig. 93)*
EDMONDSTOWN
HOUSE

*(fig. 94)*
EDMONDSTOWN HOUSE

Edmondstown House is a very rare example of High Victorian Gothic architecture in County Roscommon *(fig. 92)*. It was built in 1864 to the designs of the Dublin-born architect John McCurdy (1823-85), who was architect to the Board of Trinity College Dublin, and worked mainly in the Dublin area. He was president of the Royal Institute of the Architects of Ireland from 1875-85. The overall form of the house reflects the style: with its asymmetric composition, projecting gabled bay, corner pyramidal-roofed turret, and the steeply-pitched roof with *(fig. 93)*. The decorative elements including the horizontal bands of brick, the patterned slates in the roof and the pointed-arch window openings are also indicative of the style *(fig. 94)*.

Clonalis in Castlerea is built in a very different Victorian style. The house was built around 1880 as the new seat of the O Conor Don family, ancient landowners of the county and descendants of the last High King of Ireland. The house was built to the designs of the English architect Frederick Pepys Cockerell (1833-78). It is two storey over basement with an attic storey *(figs. 95-96)*. It is built in a hybrid of Victorian Italianate and 'Queen Anne' villa styles and is an early example in Ireland of a house built in mass concrete. The original concrete shuttering still survives on the estate. The house is open to the public and holds a unique collection of manuscripts, artifacts and family records.

*(fig. 95)*
CLONALIS HOUSE
Castlerea
Entrance Front
(c. 1878)

The house, built for the O'Conor Don family, was the first in Ireland to be constructed of mass concrete and was designed by F. Pepys Cockerell. It follows a style that is halfway between Victorian Italianate and Queen Anne that was made popular in the late 1870s and 1880s.

*(fig. 96)*
CLONALIS HOUSE
Castlerea
Garden Front

*(fig. 97)*
**Footbridge**
**Clonalis House**
**Castlerea**

An exceptional country
residence, its setting is
enhanced by the walled
garden, outbuildings,
bridges and entrance
gates.

*(fig. 98)*
Footbridge
Clonalis House
Castlerea

*(fig. 99)*
**CLONALIS HOUSE**
Castlerea

Crest showing an arm in
armour embowed holding
a sword.

*(fig. 100)*
CARRIGARD HOUSE
Boyle
(c. 1820)

The features of this sub-
stantial nineteenth-century
dwelling, particularly the
quoins and decorative
arched entrance, place
the building firmly in the
formal tradition. Two-
storeyed houses, with
central hallway, rounded
doorway and two cen-
tralised chimneys were
built from the eighteenth
century onwards. They
were often built for
traders and professional
people including clergy.

In the years following the famine period, there was a change in the nature of landholding in the country. Due to the collapse of rentals, and following the period of expansion of the eighteenth and early nineteenth centuries, some landholders became bankrupt and were forced to sell their estates under the Encumbered Estates Act (1849). This allowed for the breaking up of larger estates and the emergence of smaller holdings. In turn, this led to an increase in the building of substantial middle-sized farm houses.

A distinct architectural type emerged for this size of rural house. Its chief characteristic is that it is three bay, two storey, with a hipped roof. These houses can have rendered façades, such as Carrigard *(fig. 100)* near Boyle, or they can be stone-faced, such as Letfordspark *(fig. 101)*, also near Boyle. A distinctive feature of many of these houses is the rusticated window surrounds, which contrast with the treatment of the elevation, as can be seen in Carrigard. Variations can occur to the basic design of the house in the form of different styles of doors and entrances, and in the type of windows. Both of these attractive houses, although built on a comparatively modest scale, have been finished to a very high standard. They have also, fortunately, been well maintained and are important examples of this building type.

*(fig. 101)*
LETFORDSPARK HOUSE
Boyle
(c. 1820)

The architectural form of
the house, enhanced by
the survival of many original features and materials,
is similar to neighbouring
Carrigard House.
Letfordspark House forms
a group with the related
outbuildings, lodge and
entrance gates.

*(fig. 102)*
**Vernacular House**
**Tonvey**
**(c. 1860)**

This inhabited farmhouse is a fine example of local traditional building technology. The incorporation of thatch, corrugated-iron and asbestos cement tiles reflects the development and usage of roofing materials that has occurred over the past century.

By far the greatest number of people lived in small houses and cabins. A fine example of a rural vernacular thatched farmhouse, in excellent condition, can be found in the townland of Tonvey, in the south of the county. It is a classic four-bay, single-storey type, in which the accommodation was divided into three compartments: a large kitchen in the middle, and a bedroom at each end *(fig. 102)*. It is abutted, in a continuous line, by a two-storey outbuilding to the north and a single-storey outbuilding to the south - another classic feature of vernacular farmhouses *(fig. 103)*.

In the years following the Great Famine, there was a decline in rural population, substantially due to emigration, but there was also a growth in the population of towns *(fig. 105)*. Of course, towns had been growing since the beginning of the nineteenth century, and an early example of a nineteenth-century town dwelling can be found at Roosky *(fig. 106)*. It is a detached, irregular-plan house, originally built c. 1820. Its early date is reflected in the way it is built 'sideways-on' to the adjoining

*(fig. 103)*
**Vernacular House**
**Tonvey**

View from the rear.

(fig. 104)
**Vernacular House
Carnagh East
(c. 1840)**

This thatched house is a
rare example in County
Roscommon and is fortu-
nately well maintained.

(fig. 105)
**Main Street
Roscommon
(c. 1880-1900)**

*Courtesy of the National
Library of Ireland.*

(fig. 106)
**MOUNT CARMEL
GUEST HOUSE
Roosky
(c. 1820)**

This house addresses the
River Shannon rather than
the street. The offset
chimneystack with terra-
cotta pots is an interesting feature that has
remained.

road; it addresses the river rather than the road. Also of interest is the fine angled chimneystack, with terracotta pots. The house is adjoined by a later terrace. A later town dwelling-scheme of c. 1850 in Athleague shows how the type evolved *(fig. 107)*. The pair of terraced two- and three-bay houses is in a much simplified form, and directly addresses the street.

As towns grew in the nineteenth century, there was a commensurate rise in trade and a growth of the middle classes. A surviving early nineteenth-century shop is J.J. Tuohy's in Castlerea *(fig. 108)*. The shop (now disused) is combined with a private dwelling in a substantial three-bay, three-storey terraced scheme. The intact façade retains the fine Wyatt windows, block-and-start door surround and the original petal fanlight.

*(fig. 107)*
**Houses**
**Athleague**
**(c. 1850)**

These houses, occupying an imposing location in the village of Athleague, make a positive addition to the streetscape. The retention of much original fabric including sash windows and stone sills in conjunction with the rear outbuildings further enhances these structures.

*(fig. 108)*
**J.J. TOUHY**
**Main Street**
**Castlerea**
**(c. 1800)**

Although it is part of a terrace of urban houses, the design of J.J. Touhy's has been elevated from its neighbours through the inclusion of tripartite windows, block-and-start door surround and a petal fanlight. The intact façade boasts six-over-six timber sash windows as well as an attractive shopfront.

Ballaghaderreen is a lively market town which retains a good variety of shopfronts. M. Dooney, of about 1830, on Main Street is an excellent example of a modest terraced shop *(fig. 109)*. It retains much of its original fabric, such as the timber sash-windows, the timber double doors, and the fascia, with attractive lettering, surmounted by a finely carved cornice. Another Ballaghaderreen shop, B. Mulligan & Co., of around 1890, retains (despite some modern alterations) some fine original features. Most striking are the beautiful curved-glass display windows, with stained glass overlights *(fig. 110)*, and the attractive mosaic threshold with the name of the original shop, Flannery's *(fig. 111)*.

(fig. 109)
M. DOONEY
Main Street
Ballaghaderreen
(c. 1830)

It is typical of mid nineteenth-century shopfronts found in Irish towns and villages. The attractive lettering to the fascia, surmounted by a finely carved cornice, enhances the building and is a positive contribution to the character of the streetscape.

(fig. 110)
B. MULLIGAN & CO.
Main Street/Market
Street
Ballaghaderreen
(c. 1890)

B. Mulligan's, situated on the busy main street and formerly known as Flannery's, has retained its original form and proportion. The display windows curve into the entrance with a mosaic threshold and stained glass detailing, which are a colourful and interesting addition to the building.

(fig. 111)
B. MULLIGAN & CO.

Detail of 'Flannery' mosaic threshold.

*(fig. 112)*
**Former bank**
**Church Street/Market**
**Place**
**Strokestown**
**(c. 1850)**

The stucco detailing employed in the execution of the quoins, opening surrounds and elaborate doorway add an artistic element to this significant building. Built to classical proportions this former bank contributes to the architectural heritage of the area.

*(fig. 113)*
**BANK OF IRELAND**
**Church Street**
**Strokestown**
**(c. 1890)**

Strokestown's Bank of Ireland is one of the few red brick structures in the town. Its brickwork, limestone dressings and timber eaves brackets create a pleasant architectural scheme.

*(fig. 114)*
**BANK OF IRELAND**
**Church Street**
**Strokestown**

Detail showing Corinthian style colonnette.

Economic improvement, from the growth of agriculture and trade, along with the rise of a middle class, led to an increase in the circulation of money. Banks and post offices were buildings which emerged as new architectural types in the second half of the nineteenth century. Two examples of nineteenth-century bank architecture are to be seen in Strokestown. The former bank of about 1850 on Church Street conveys the importance of the financial institution in its proportions and its robust classical detailing *(fig. 112)*. The adjoining Bank of Ireland, built in about 1890, is very different in character *(fig. 113)*. Its red brick walls, bracketed eaves, segmental-headed windows and, in particular, the Venetian Gothic foliate capitals, are all typical features of the period *(fig. 114)*. In fact, the proportion and form of the building, with the hipped roof, gives the bank the character of a semi-detached house.

As in the eighteenth century, there was a need for buildings of law and order: barracks and courthouses. The former courthouse in Castlerea is a particularly fine example. Built in 1852, it is an impressive building conveying authority and control *(fig. 115)*. Despite its scale, it has finely carved details such as cut-stone quoins and moulded architraves *(fig. 116)*. It was possibly designed by William Caldbeck, as it follows a standard courthouse design associated with him. However, drawings in the National Archives suggest it might have been built to the design of a Godfrey Willis. Now used as county council offices, it is a very important building in the townscape of Castlerea. Ballaghaderreen has a good example of a nineteenth-century barracks building.

*(fig. 115)*
ROSCOMMON COUNTY
COUNCIL OFFICE
(former courthouse)
Main Street
Castlerea
(c. 1840)

This former courthouse follows a standard design associated with William Caldbeck. The use of limestone dressings heightens the architectural impact.

*(fig. 116)*
ROSCOMMON COUNTY
COUNCIL OFFICE
(former courthouse)
Main Street
Castlerea

*(fig. 117)*
KILTULLAGH CHURCH
OF IRELAND
Ballinlough
(1818)

Built in 1818, this church
is a focal point within the
village of Ballinlough.
The architect, Thomas
Cosgrove, positioned the
church so that it could be
viewed from all four roads
leading into the town.

*(fig. 118)*
KILTULLAGH CHURCH
OF IRELAND CHURCH
Ballinlough

The nineteenth century was a very active period for church-building - both Roman Catholic and Church of Ireland. Although the Board of First Fruits (the source of funds for Church of Ireland building) was established in the eighteenth century, the most active period of building was between 1800 and 1830. The classic Board of First Fruits church was almost uniform in its architectural character. They were simple single-cell structures with a castellated tower and sometimes with a spire. They were nearly always carefully and picturesquely sited, and are a familiar feature in the Irish landscape.

A good example can be found at Ballinlough, where the church is like a citadel, on an elevated site, the focal point of the village *(fig. 117)*. It has a very simple exterior, a pair of lancet windows to each side of the nave and the castellated tower with pinnacles forming the west front. The interior is simple and unassuming; it has a timber open-truss roof and the decoration is mostly restricted to the stained-glass windows *(fig. 118)*. It was built in 1818, at a cost of £2,500, to the design of architect Thomas Cosgrove.

(fig. 119)
**HOLY TRINITY CHURCH
OF IRELAND CHURCH**
Croghan
(c. 1810)

The church is sited in an elevated and picturesque location.

A different arrangement can be found in the elegant Holy Trinity church at Croghan, also of 1818. Here the nave is four bays, the tower is engaged and has a spire, and there is a projecting chancel to the east *(figs. 119-120)*. The building is of coursed limestone throughout. The church at Dunamon erected in 1854 shows how the design of Church of Ireland churches

(fig. 120)
**HOLY TRINITY CHURCH
OF IRELAND CHURCH**
Croghan

The stepped base leads to an octagonal tower and then forms a pointed spire.

*(fig. 121)*
**DUNAMON CHURCH OF
IRELAND CHURCH
(1854)**

Set back from a quiet
country road within its
own grounds, Dunamon
Church of Ireland church
is a well-proportioned and
handsomely decorated
structure.

*(fig. 122)*
**DUNAMON CHURCH OF
IRELAND CHURCH**

Well-finished cast-iron
windows and doors
enriched by studs and
hinges compliment the
dressed limestone
elevations.

(fig. 123)
ST MARY'S ROMAN
CATHOLIC CHURCH
Keadew
(c. 1860)

evolved during the nineteenth century *(fig. 121)*. It was designed by the Cork-born architect, Joseph Welland (1798-1860), who was the main architect for the Established Church from 1831 onwards, designing more than one hundred churches around the country *(fig. 122)*. The handsome design shows the influence of the noted English architect and polemicist, A.W.N. Pugin. Despite Pugin's associations with Catholic church architecture, his architectural principles began to be incorporated into Established church designs from the middle of the century. These principles included an emphasis on the chancel, the incorporation of south porches, baptisteries and open timber roofs, the pursuit of 'honest' construction, and the use of stained glass. As can be seen at Dunamon, Puginian churches were frequently single-cell with the tower replaced by a bellcote.

The nineteenth century was also a great era for Roman Catholic church building. Although Catholic Relief Acts were passed from 1778, full Catholic Emancipation was not granted until 1829. This encouraged, if not immediately, a coherent church-building programme.

A fine example in county Roscommon is St Mary's, Keadew *(fig. 123)*. It was built about 1860 to the designs of J.J. McCarthy (1817-82), the prolific Irish Catholic church architect. Like the Church of Ireland church at Dunamon, mentioned already, St Mary's also reflects the theories of A.W.N. Pugin, who was so influential in liturgical and architectural theory. Indeed, McCarthy was known as the 'Irish Pugin'. The church strikingly appropriates the Board of First Fruits tradition of careful scenographic location. Here the church is on an elevated site a short distance outside the village but visible for miles around.

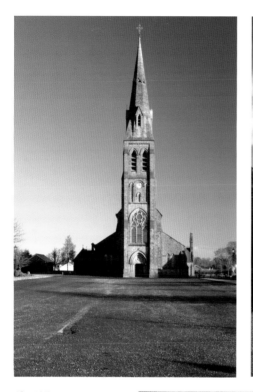

(fig. 125)
THE ANNUNCIATION
AND ST NATHY
Pound Street/Cathedral
Street
Ballaghaderreen

(fig. 124)
THE ANNUNCIATION
AND ST NATHY
Pound Street/Cathedral
Street
Ballaghaderreen
(1855-1860)

The west front of
the Ballaghaderreen
Cathedral, with its soaring
central tower and spire, is
flanked on either side
with lower lean-to aisles.

(fig. 126)
THE ANNUNCIATION
AND ST NATHY

The rock-faced masonry
and carved limestone
dressings enhance the
cathedral's architectural
form and are clearly the
work of skilled craftsmen.

(fig. 127)
THE ANNUNCIATION
AND ST NATHY

View looking towards the
altar and the traceried
east window. The arcades
with simple capitals,
which divide the nave
from the aisles, are of
Scottish sandstone and
rest on plain cylindrical
granite piers. The bases
and shafts of the piers are
of local blue limestone.

*(fig. 128)*
**DÚN MAEVE (former convent)**
**Strokestown**
**(c. 1900)**

The variety of materials employed such as tooled stone, rock-faced stonework and yellow brick is of technical interest. Additional features including single, double and triple light windows provide a rhythm to the façade.

*(fig. 129)*
**MARY IMMACULATE SECONDARY SCHOOL**
**Convent Road**
**Roscommon**
**(1854)**

The nuns' graveyard with highly ornate ironwork completes the setting with the convent.

*(fig. 130)*
**MARY IMMACULATE SECONDARY SCHOOL**

The Cathedral of the Annunciation and St Nathy in Ballaghaderreen is built to an idiosyncratic design. It is a curious mixture of styles with a very imposing spire and was substantially complete in 1860 *(figs. 124-127)*. It was designed by an English firm of architects, Hadfield & Goldie. The spire, added in 1912, is the work of W.H. Byrne of Dublin.

The Catholic building campaign also included monasteries and convents. A typical example of late nineteenth-century convent architecture can be found in Strokestown *(fig. 128)*.

Churches of other denominations, also built during the nineteenth century, are generally simple, but finished to a high degree. The Presbyterian church (1858) in Boyle is a fine scheme *(fig. 131)*. Even though it is modest in scale, its elevated site gives it a commanding presence. A fine Presbyterian church also survives in Roscommon town *(fig. 132)*. The church is simply composed but incorporates elegant and restrained classical proportions and details with highly skilled stonework. It was erected in 1865. The former Methodist church in Boyle is built in a most unusual style *(fig. 133)*. Built c. 1890, the church is now no longer used. With its barrel-shaped corrugated-iron roof, it is a good and rare example of the type.

(fig. 131)
BOYLE FEDERAL
CHURCH
Carrick Road
Boyle
(1858)

As a centre of worship, which is used both by the Presbyterian and Methodist congregations in Boyle, the Federal Church is socially significant.

*(fig. 132)*
DR JOHN HARRISON
MEMORIAL HALL
(former Presbyterian
Church)
The Square
Roscommon
(1863)

This former Presbyterian
church, whose construc-
tion was funded by a
Michael Sherra, is one of
a number of buildings of
high architectural quality
set around the square.
The 'Star of David' win-
dow, which represents
The Trinity, is particularly
notable and is said by
local tradition to com-
memorate the Welsh
builders. The cast-iron
railings and gates com-
plete the setting of this
architecturally significant
building.

*(fig. 133)*
BOYLE METHODIST
CHURCH
Main Street
Boyle
(c. 1890)

The Methodists first
obtained a lease for their
meeting house in 1793.
The unusual style and use
of corrugated iron in the
construction of this building makes it an interest-
ing part of the town's
architectural heritage.

# The Twentieth Century

Following the turbulent years of the first decades of the twentieth century, the Irish Free State was established in 1922. Amongst the first priorities of the new regime was a programme of infrastructural projects - water, electricity, social housing and schools. The twentieth century was not, therefore, an era of grand architectural statements.

Like most counties in the west of Ireland, Roscommon suffered from a continuous decline in population for most of the century. While the majority of settlement remained rural and town structures generally remained small, some new residential building did occur in urban areas.

An example of new building in the heart of a village can be found in Keadew *(fig. 134)*. The semi-detached unit was built circa 1920. It is a fine composition which terminates the northern vista of the village. Each house is two storey with three bays and the front door is centrally placed with a canted bay window to either side. The pair of houses is unified by the single-span hipped roof. The houses are distinctly 'urban' in character, opening directly onto the road.

In the vicinity of the bigger towns it is possible to see the emergence of the suburban-type house, for example in the eastern outskirts of Castlerea. Shown here are examples from Carrick-on-Shannon (c. 1920) and Strokestown (c. 1940). The pair of semi-detached houses in Carrick-on-Shannon *(fig. 135)* is broadly similar in form to the scheme in Keadew (hipped roof, two storey, each house of three bays with a centrally placed door) yet, overall, the two schemes are very different. Where the broad expanse of the houses in Keadew give the appearance of a terrace, the houses in Carrick are much more compact, and thus form a more distinct 'pair'. Most significantly, the Carrick houses are separated from the road by a front garden - a key feature of suburban housing. Other typically suburban elements are the bow windows, the pebbledash render, and the perimeter wall with pedestrian gates.

The semi-detached houses in Strokestown show a further evolution of the suburban type *(fig. 136)*. Here the façade of each house is asymmetrical: there are two bays on the first floor, three on the ground. The entrance is to the side, recessed behind an open porch, and

*(fig. 134)*
**Houses**
**Keadew**
**(c. 1920)**

This early twentieth-century pair makes a positive contribution to the streetscape, terminating the vista at the north-western end of the town. The pleasing symmetry and decorative canted bay windows combine to create a simple and elegant architectural design, further enhanced by the retention of many original materials.

*(fig. 136)*
**House**
**Strokestown**
**(c. 1940)**

*(fig. 135)*
**House**
**Carrick-on-Shannon**
**(c. 1920)**

This house is particularly noteworthy with the retention of its original windows. The wrought-iron gates enhance the setting of the houses.

*(fig. 137)*
JAMES MULLANY
Main Street
Boyle
(c. 1870, shopfront
c. 1940)

The vitrolite shopfront,
with chrome trim and the
plastic lettering to the
fascia, is intact at
Mullany's.

*(fig. 138)*
SHEERIN'S
Patrick Street
Boyle
(c. 1860, shopfront
c. 1940)

*(fig. 139)*
ROSCOMMON POST
OFFICE
The Square
Roscommon
(1911)

The warm red hue of the
façade contrasts with the
predominantly limestone
or rendered buildings
on the square. Its early
twentieth-century design
and detailing is articulated
by the ashlar limestone
dressings and other
decorative features such
as the tooled stone
post box.

there is a full-height bow, surmounted by a pediment breaking through the roof line. A stucco platband separates the ground and first floor. These houses are a fine composition and typical of the best semi-detached house design of the mid-twentieth century. The retention of the original timber casement windows adds greatly to the interest of these houses.

Despite their relatively small size, the towns remained important market centres. In the 1930s and 40s, a common feature of the busier towns around the county, such as Boyle, Castlerea and Ballaghaderreen, was the 'upgrading' of existing shops by the addition of new, modern fronts. This can be seen in two examples in Boyle: Mullany's on Main Street *(fig. 137)* and Sheerin's on Patrick Street *(fig. 138)*. Both shopfronts are faced in sleek black vitriolite with chrome dressings, and incorporate clear, streamlined lettering for the names. They are good examples of the 'moderne' style which, once so popular, has now become quite rare in Ireland.

Following the proliferation of banks from the early nineteenth century, purpose-built post offices emerged in many of the larger towns towards the end of the century. This building campaign continued into the twentieth century. Mostly built by the Office of Public Works, they are fine examples of modest provincial public architecture.

The post office in Roscommon town was built in 1911 to designs by Harold G. Leask (1882-1964), an Office of Public Works architect *(fig. 139)*. He was also a pioneering architectural historian, who published seminal works on Irish castles, churches and monastic buildings. The post office is detached, two storeys with five bays, with the end bays projecting, and a hipped roof. It is built in red brick in a neo-Georgian style. The chief feature is the timber sash-windows, the end bays being emphasised by tripartite windows. There are limestone details, such as the string course and the monumental door surround *(fig. 140)*.

*(fig. 140)*
Detail of doorway.

*(fig. 141)*
**BOYLE POST OFFICE**
Carrick Road
**Boyle**
(c. 1910)

Boyle's red brick post office is a colourful addition to the streetscape, retaining many original features and materials.

*(fig. 142)*
Post Box
**Boyle**
(c. 1905)

This Edward VII post box is simple in design with decorative detailing on cap and pillar. The execution of the elaborate intertwined raised lettering and crown adds an artistic aspect to this functional object.

*(fig. 143)*
Post Box
**Cloverhill**
(c. 1905)

This wall-mounted post box is particularly notable for the combination of elements dating from the nineteenth and early twentieth centuries.

The post office in Boyle was built between 1910-20 and was designed by G.W. Crowe, another Office of Public Works architect *(fig. 141)*. It has a more modern spare style. It is a fine composition: detached, three bay and three storeys with flanking two-storey entrance bays. The monumentality of the building is emphasised by the substantial limestone parapet that hides the roof. Again, the building is brick, which continues around the side elevations, but the façade of the ground floor is distinguished by channelled render.

Post boxes are an important part of the street furniture of towns and villages and immediately evoke the period in which they were erected. Unfortunately, they are under threat, and fast disappearing. There is an early twentieth-century example in Boyle, dating to the reign of King Edward VII *(fig. 142)*. The elaborate intertwining of the initials is particularly attractive. An indication of the political changes which occurred in the early twentieth century can be found in an unusual post box in the village of Cloverhill *(fig. 143)*. It has the insignia of King Edward VII but the original door was replaced after the establishment of the new Irish Government; the new door incorporates a harp and the initials SÉ, to represent 'Saorstát Éireann', the Irish Free State.

The Church of the Sacred Heart in Roscommon town, consecrated in 1903, was the most significant church to be built in the county in the twentieth century *(figs. 144-146)*. Also known as the Gillooley Memorial Church, it is an immense and imposing structure, set on an elevated site and is richly composed of limestone with sandstone dressings and fine stained glass throughout. According to local sources, it was designed by P.J. Kilgallen

of Sligo who worked for Bishop Gillooley on other projects. The contractor was Thomas Lee of Longford. The asymmetrical façade is dominated by the tower (which was added in 1916 to designs by O'Callaghan & Webb) and by the magnificent rose window, which depicts the patron saint of every diocese in Ireland. The rose window is the culmination of the thirty-three invocations of the Sacred Heart, which are the subject of the sixteen clerestory windows around the church. At the beginning of the twentieth century, this was seen as the first attempt to illustrate the new Litany of the Sacred Heart in stained glass.

St Joseph's Church in Boyle is a striking modern composition *(fig. 147)*. Built in 1980, it reflects the modernising principles of the Second Vatican Council (1962-65). It is circular in plan and its battered walls are clad in random-coursed limestone. The entrance porch is defined by a substantial monolithic buttressing wall. The church has a low domed roof and the whole structure is evocative of an early Christian stone fort or cashel. Inside, the roof is a beautiful timber structure, with slender ribs radiating from the central apex. With the plain glass windows appearing to 'support' the soaring roof, the interior is spacious, light and peaceful.

The provision of a primary schooling to all children was embarked upon in the early nineteenth century, with the establishment of the National Board of Education in 1806. From the 1830s, national schools were built throughout rural Ireland. Highlake School, dating from 1857, is a fine example. Now a private dwelling, it is a compact, three bay, single storey structure and is enlivened by the central copper turret and the gable front over the cen-

Ballymun Branch. Tel. 8421890

*(fig. 144)*
**SACRED HEART ROMAN
CATHOLIC CHURCH**
**Abbey Street**
**Roscommon**
**(1903)**

The combination of
rock-faced walls and
fine sandstone dressings
provides interesting
textural contrast.

*(fig. 145)*
**SACRED HEART ROMAN CATHOLIC CHURCH**
**Abbey Street**
**Roscommon**

View looking towards the altar with the rood screen above. The artistic execution of the carved detailing, mosaics, stained glass and interior decoration complement and enhance this imposing church.

*(fig. 146)*
**SACRED HEART ROMAN CATHOLIC CHURCH**
**Abbey Street**
**Roscommon**

View looking towards the east end gallery with the rose window above.

*(fig. 147)*
**ST JOSEPH'S ROMAN CATHOLIC CHURCH**
**Boyle**
**(1980)**

This visually striking church is built in the style of a defensive early Christian period cashel. Its battered walls are typical of such monuments. Once inside the church, the open roof and the prevalence of light and space, create a peaceful and contemplative atmosphere.

*(fig. 148)*
**ST NATHY'S COLLEGE**
**Main Street**
**Ballaghaderreen**
**(1916)**

St Nathy's College comprises a school, a former barracks and a gate lodge. The barracks was established c. 1830 and the school was built in 1916. The architectural design of the school is articulated by the ornate stucco detailing and rhythmical fenestration.

*(fig. 149)*
**BALLINTOBER NATIONAL SCHOOL**
**Ballintober**
**(1929)**

This former national school, built in 1929, retains much original fabric such as the slate roof, sash windows, cast-iron roof vents and rainwater goods.

*(fig. 150)*
**BALLINTOBER NATIONAL SCHOOL**
**Ballintober**

(fig. 152)

(fig. 151)
FORMER CASTLEREA
VOCATIONAL COLLEGE
St Patrick's Street
Castlerea
(c. 1950)

The form and scale of this former vocational school are representative of the architectural designs employed by the state for buildings of this type. The simple form and rhythmical fenestration of the building combine to create a pleasant exterior, which is fitting for a centre of education.

tral bay. The square-headed windows on the front elevation extend up into the roof line and would have provided a bright interior.

The provision of schools was a renewed concern and a major priority for the new state. The design of the national schools in the twentieth century was more standardised. A typical example is Ballintober National School, erected in 1929 *(figs. 149-150)*. The building is built on a T-plan, with projecting bays flanking a central gable-fronted entrance porch, which form reflects the separate schooling of boys and girls. An attractive feature of the building

is the original timber sash-windows whose rhythm and glazing bars unite the variably sized windows.

The former vocational school at Castlerea of around 1950 is on a very different scale to the domestic proportions of the national schools *(fig. 151)*. The height of the two-storey building is emphasised by the tall proportion of the windows and the deep eaves. The regular rhythm of the elevations is emphasised by the grid of the glazing bars of the sash-windows *(fig. 152)*.

The early years of the new state saw a development of local industries as part of the drive for national self-sufficiency. The weir and sluice-gates erected in Castlerea in the 1920s is an example of this effort *(figs. 153-154)*. The neighbouring double-span footbridge with cast-iron railings now leads to a public park, developed on the demesne of the Sandford family, after it sold its estate to the Town Trust *(fig. 155)*.

The provision and building of social and leisure facilities became a characteristic of the century. From the 1930s onwards, the cinema became a hugely popular form of entertainment throughout Ireland. By the early 1940s there were cinemas in Boyle, Ballaghaderreen , Roscommon and Strokestown. Like many of the more modest cinemas around the country,

the one in Roscommon has been closed and is now used as a night-club *(fig. 156)*. Although simple in form and small in scale, the design bears the influence of the Modern Movement, particularly in the concrete canopy over the entrance, the polished granite of the façade and the streamlined circular ticket-booth.

A delightful eye-catcher cottage in Ballydangan, built as an ice-cream parlour in the mid-1930s, also reflects the increase in leisure time *(fig. 157)*. Now largely overgrown by vegetation, the building has a curved gable front, with a round window above a central doorway flanked by harp-shaped windows. Although a modest rural building, its striking incorporation of the harp would have been a potent symbol of national independence.

*(fig. 153)*
Weir and sluice gates
Castlerea
(c. 1920)

This stone weir complete with its sluice gates formed part of a group of structures associated with a water mill. The survival of these structures together with the footbridge makes an interesting contribution to the architectural and industrial heritage of the town.

*(fig. 154)*
Weir and sluice gates
Castlerea

*(fig. 155)*
**Footbridge
Castlerea**

*(fig. 156)*
**THE ROYAL
Castle Street
Roscommon
(c. 1940)**

This cinema is typical of mid-twentieth-century architecture. Inspired by the Modern Movement, the design of the ticket booth is stylish, being enlivened by features and fabrics including cement render and granite.

*(fig. 157)*
**MOORE
Ballydangan
(c. 1940)**

This idiosyncratic mid-twentieth century structure is a celebration of Irishness. The modest style, which appears to have been influenced by contemporary modern design, is happily elevated by unusual harp-shaped windows, colourful tiles and bright paintwork.

# Conclusion

(fig. 158)
Water pump
Castlecoote
(c. 1850)

The buildings and artefacts included in this essay are only a representative sample of the entire National Inventory of Architectural Heritage survey of Roscommon. They have been selected for a variety of reasons, such as for archaeological, architectural, historical, industrial, engineering or technical interest. It is intended that they reflect the built heritage of County Roscommon as a whole.

The built heritage of Ireland is uniquely important as a testament to our national and local history and is fundamentally intertwined with it. Hence we see the fortifications of Shannonbridge, built out of fear of potential invasion during the Napoleonic era; the mill at Castlerea, which was so important in the evolution of the town; the alterations to an Edwardian post box to reflect the establishment of the new state.

The built heritage of the country is far more than big or grand buildings. There is a wide variety of structures and sites in the survey: it includes churches, railway stations, farm buildings, country houses, mills and bridges. These everyday buildings, structures and artefacts give the country its character and identity. Also very important to note and protect are the smaller artefacts, such as water-pumps *(fig. 158)*, post boxes, gateways, railings, cobbles and pavings. The towns of Roscommon contain fine examples of traditional local shopfronts. However, it is just as important to protect and conserve the distinctive and elegant mosaic or vitriolite frontages of the thirties and forties, which are frequently replaced by pastiche traditional façades.

Ireland's built heritage is subject to ongoing challenges. These include ill-advised alterations, abandonment or even demolition of historic buildings. In Roscommon, as elsewhere, there are found sadly decayed churches and houses, large and small, which have survived undamaged for over two centuries, and now are lying empty and in danger of serious decay or insensitive alteration. However, cause for real optimism is the restoration of Elphin windmill and the saving of the magnificent King House in Boyle. With increasing awareness and care, we can retain and celebrate our local built heritage as a legacy for the future.

# Further Reading

Aalen, F.H.A., Kevin Whelan and Matthew Stout (eds), *Atlas of the Irish Rural Landscape* (Cork, 1997).

Bence-Jones, Mark, *A Guide to Irish Country Houses* (London, 1988).

Coleman, Anne, *Riotous Roscommon: Social unrest in the 1840s* (Dublin, 1999).

Craig, Maurice, *Buildings and sites of historic/artistic interest in County Roscommon* (An Foras Forbatha, Dublin, 1976).

Craig, Maurice, *Classic Irish Houses of the Middle Size* (London, 1976).

Craig, Maurice, *The Architecture of Ireland from the earliest times to 1880* (London and Dublin, 1989).

De Breffny, Brian and Rosemary ffolliott, *The Houses of Ireland* (London, 1975).

Duffy, Sean (ed.), *Atlas of Irish History* (Dublin, 1997).

FitzGerald, Desmond, The Knight of Glin, David J. Griffin and Nicholas K. Robinson, *Vanishing Country Houses of Ireland* (Dublin, 1988).

Foster, Roy (ed.), *The Oxford Illustrated History of Ireland* (London, 1989).

Graham, B.J. and L.J. Proudfoot, *An Historical Geography of Ireland* (London, 1993).

Grose, Francis, *The Antiquities of Ireland*, 2 vols (London, 1791-95).

Harbison, Peter, *Guide to National and Historic Monuments of Ireland* (Dublin, 1992).

Howley, James, *The Follies and Garden Buildings of Ireland* (New Haven and London, 1993).

Kerrigan, Paul, *Castles and Fortifications in Ireland 1485-1945* (Cork, 1995).

Leask, H.G., *Irish Castles* (Dundalk, 1941; reprinted 1973).

Leask, H.G., *Irish Churches and Monastic Buildings*, 3 vols (Dundalk, 1955-60).

Lewis, Samuel, *A Topographical Dictionary of Ireland,* 2 vols (London, 1837; reprinted Galway, 1995).

Mattimoe, Cyril, *North Roscommon - its people and past* (Boyle, 1992).

Moody, T.W. and F.X. Martin (eds), *The Course of Irish History* (Dublin, 2001).

Roscommon County *Development Plan,* 2 vols (1993).

Rothery, Sean, *A Field Guide to the Buildings of Ireland* (Dublin, 1997).

Weld, Isaac, *A Statistical Survey of the County of Roscommon* (Dublin, 1832).

Wheeler, Gordon, 'John Nash and the building of Rockingham, Co. Roscommon' in Terence Reeves-Smyth and Richard Oram (eds), *Avenues to the Past: Essays presented to Sir Charles Brett on his 75th year* (Belfast, 2003).

Worsley, Giles, 'Strokestown Park, Co. Roscommon', in *Country Life* (1 April 1993), pp. 56-59.

Young, Arthur, *A tour in Ireland*, 2 vols (London, 1780).

# Registration Numbers

*The structures mentioned in the text of this Introduction are listed below. It is possible to find more information on each structure by accessing our survey on the Internet at* **www.buildingsofireland.ie** *and searching by the Registration Number. Structures are listed by page number.*

56-57 Cloontykilla Castle
Former Rockingham Demesne
*Reg. 31906039*

58-59 Fairy Bridge
Former Rockingham Demesne
*Reg. 31906007*

58-59 Fishing lodge
Former Rockingham Demesne
Reg. 31906002

59 Gate lodge
Ballintober
*Reg. 31934004*

60 Clock tower
The Crescent
Boyle
*Reg. 31804055*

60-61 Carrowroe Park
Carrowroe
*Reg. 31940002*

62 Edmondstown House
Edmondstown
*Reg. 31908001*

63 Clonalis House
Castlerea
*Reg. 31920004*

65 Footbridge
Clonalis House
Castlerea
*Reg. 31920004*

65 Carrigard House
Boyle
*Reg. 31906029*

65 Letfordspark
Boyle
*Reg. 31906028*

66 Vernacular house
Tonvey
*Reg. 31954005*

67 Vernacular House
Carnagh East
*Reg. 31946001*

66-67 Mount Carmel guesthouse
Roosky
*Reg. 31812002*

68 House
Athleague
Reg. 31822007

68 J.J. Touhy
Main Street
Castlerea
*Reg. 31814020*

69 M. Dooney
Main Street
Ballaghaderreen
*Reg. 31805007*

69 B. Mulligan & Co.
Main Street/Market Street
Ballaghaderreen
*Reg. 31805011*

70-71 Former bank
Church Street/Market Place
Strokestown
*Reg. 31811012*

70-71 Bank of Ireland
Church Street
Strokestown
*Reg. 31811011*

71 Roscommon County Council
office (former courthouse)
Main Street
Castlerea
*Reg. 31814030*

72 Kiltullagh Church of
Ireland Church
Ballinlough
*Reg. 31813002*

73 Holy Trinity Church of
Ireland Church
Croghan
*Reg. 31806006*

73-75 Dunamon Church of
Ireland Church
*Reg. 31938005*

75 St Mary's Roman
Catholic Church
Keadew
*Reg. 31803005*

76-77 The Annunciation and
St Nathy
Pound Street/Cathedral Street
Ballaghaderreen
*Reg. 31805020*

77 Dún Maeve (former convent)
Strokestown
*Reg. 31811001*

77 Mary Immaculate
Secondary School
Convent Road
Roscommon
*Reg. 31817036*

78 Boyle Federal Church
Carrick Road
Boyle
*Reg. 31804051*

78-79 Dr John Harrison
Memorial Hall
(former Presbyterian Church)
The Square
Roscommon
*Reg. 31817011*

78-79 Boyle Methodist Church
Main Street
Boyle
*Reg. 31804008*

80-81 Houses
Keadew
*Reg. 31803004*

80-81 House
Carrick-on-Shannon
*Reg. 31811004*

80-81 House
Strokestown
*Reg. 31811004*

82-83 James Mullany
Main Street
Boyle
*Reg. 31804030*

82-83 Sheerin's
Patrick Street
Boyle
*Reg. 31804034*

83 Roscommon Post Office
The Square
Roscommon
*Reg. 31817010*

84-85 Boyle Post Office
Carrick Road
Boyle
*Reg. 31804048*

84-85 Post box
Boyle
*Reg. 31804014*

84-85 Post box
Cloverhill
*Reg. 31939001*

85-87 Sacred Heart Roman
Catholic Church
Abbey Street
Roscommon
*Reg. 31817034*

85, 87 St Joseph's Roman
Catholic Church
Boyle
*Reg. 31804046*

85 Highlake Monastery School
Ardlagheen More
*Reg. 31935002*

88 St Nathy's College
Main Street
Ballaghaderreen
*Reg. 31805015*

88-89 Ballintober National School
Ballintober
*Reg. 31815003*

89 Former Castlerea
Vocational College
St Patrick's Street
Castlerea
*Reg. 31814045*

90 Weir and sluice gates
Castlerea
*Reg. 31814014*

90-91 The Royal
Castle Street
Roscommon
*Reg. 31817003*

90-91 Moore
Ballydangan
*Reg. 31954004*

92 Water pump
Castlecoote
*Reg. 31816002*

# Acknowledgements

**NIAH STAFF**
Willy Cumming, Mildred Dunne, Gareth John, Mark Kehoe, Deborah Lawlor, Paul McNally, Damian Murphy, Flora O'Mahony, TJ O'Meara, Barry O'Reilly, Brendan Pocock, Marc Ritchie, Marian Ryan, Erika Sjöberg.

*The NIAH gratefully acknowledges the following in the preparation of the Roscommon County Survey and Introduction:*

**Survey Fieldwork**
Architectural Recording and Research (Bronagh Lanigan and Sinead Hughes) with Sarah-Jane Halpin, Mary-Liz McCarthy, Audrey McGrath, Catherine Murphy and Róisín Quinn.

**Introduction**
*Writer* Eve McAulay
*Editor* Willy Cumming, Mildred Dunne and Barry O'Reilly
*Copy Editor* Lucy Freeman
*Photographer* Roslyn Byrne Photography
*Designed by* Bennis Design
*Printed by* New Oceans

The NIAH wishes to thank all those who allowed access to their property for the purposes of the Roscommon County Survey and subsequent photography.

The NIAH wishes to acknowledge the generous assistance given by the staff of the Photographic Archive, Department of the Environment, Heritage and Local Government, the Irish Architectural Archive, the National Library of Ireland, the National Photographic Archive, Simmons Aerofilms Limited, and the National Archives, Kew. The assistance given by Michael Moore, Dan O'Meara and Mary O'Meara is greatly appreciated.

**Sources of Illustrations**
All of the original photography for the Introduction was taken by Roslyn Byrne. The illustrations below are identified by their figure number:

1 is courtesy of Matthew Stout; 2 courtesy of the Ordnance Survey of Ireland; 3, 4, 5, 6, 8, 21 courtesy of the Photographic Unit, Department of the Environment, Heritage and Local Government; 7, 9, 12, 24, 53, 63, 64, 87, 105 are property of the National Library of Ireland and have been reproduced with the permission of the Council of the Trustees of the National Library of Ireland; 45 is courtesy of Simmons Aerofilms Limited; 46 is courtesy of the National Archives, Kew; 65, 66, 67 courtesy of the Irish Architectural Archive.

The NIAH has made every effort to source and acknowledge the owners of all of the archival illustrations included in this Introduction. The NIAH apologies for any omissions made, and would be happy to include such acknowledgements in future issues of this Introduction.

Please note that the majority of the structures included in the Roscommon County Survey are privately owned and are therefore not open to the public.

ISBN: 0755719085
© Government of Ireland 2004

# Questionnaire

Name:

Address:

Email:

Age:   10 - 18      18 -30      30 - 50      50 - 65      65+

Occupation:

Did you purchase this publication for:   General interest          Professional use

Comments/Suggestions/Corrections:

*The information in this questionnaire is to provide a feedback to the NIAH.*
*It will be kept confidential and will not given to any other authority.*

The NIAH survey of the architectural heritage of County Roscommon can be accessed on the internet at: ***www.buildingsofireland.ie*** The data accessible on the internet includes a written record and images of each of the sites included in the NIAH survey. However, the mapping data, indicating the location of each site surveyed, is not available on the NIAH website.

**If you would like to receive the mapping on CD-ROM please complete this questionnaire and send it with a stamped addressed envelope, large enough to hold a CD, to NIAH, Dún Scéine, Harcourt Lane, Dublin 2.**